Books for Children to Read Alone

Books
for Children
to Read Alone

A Guide for Parents and Librarians

George Wilson • Joyce Moss

R. R. Bowker Company
New York & London, 1988

Published by R. R. Bowker Company
a division of Reed Publishing (USA) Inc.
Copyright © 1988 by Reed Publishing (USA) Inc.
All rights reserved
Printed and bound in the United States of America

Except as permitted under the Copyright Act of 1976,
no part of this publication may be reproduced or transmitted
in any form or by any means, or stored in any information storage
and retrieval system, without prior written permission of
R. R. Bowker Company, 245 West 17 Street, New York, NY 10011

Library of Congress Cataloging-in-Publication Data

Wilson, George, 1920–
    Books for children to read alone : a guide for parents and
librarians / George Wilson, Joyce Moss.
      p.   cm.
    Includes indexes.
    ISBN 0-8352-2346-9
    1. Children's literature—Bibliography.   2. Children—Books and
reading.   I. Moss, Joyce, 1951– . II. Title.
Z1037.W748   1988
[PN1009.A1]
011'.62—dc19   88-10430
                                        CIP

Contents

Preface

"You read to me, I'll read to you." When she was three years old, Erin already wanted to read to people as a change from being read to. Both reading and being read to are important to young people, as is the interaction it provides. Listening encourages young readers to associate aural language with the printed word and builds an interest in stories. Reading alone builds self-confidence and gives the child a feeling of achievement.

For librarians and parents there are hundreds, even thousands, of great children's books to choose from. In fact, as time passes more books are published—2,500 of them new each year. There are great books about matters that are of vital interest to children, things that are happening to them, that are written with the children's listening and speaking vocabulary in mind—a vocabulary that far outreaches the reading vocabulary of most people. Thus, it is a formidable task to select books either for reading aloud to children or for the young readers to handle on their own.

In searching through children's books for this project, we found many more of the read-to variety of books than the read-alone kind. For example, the popular folktales and fairy tales that still enchant children are, for the most part, examples of great stories that are seldom written at the level of the most interested reader. These books are, nonetheless, attractive because someone must read them to the child to whom they are conceptually geared.

Jim Trelease's *The Read Aloud Handbook* (Penguin, 1982) is an excellent starting place for the person who wants to read to young people. Our search was for those books that are, by concept and vocabulary, ones that young readers can read alone. We have designed *Books for Children to Read Alone* to be an equally valuable resource of books to involve young people in independent reading.

We wish to give special thanks to young Micaela and Jenny. Micaela reviewed the entire list and added her personal rating to each entry. Jenny also reviewed the entire list and offered her own annotations for some of the books. Both children were among the ever changing group of young readers who recommended books for the list.

We are deeply indebted to Judy Cantor, head librarian at UCLA's University Elementary School library, for helping us locate the books and providing information about the books most used in her library, and to Tracy Johnson, graduate school assistant at UCLA's University Elementary School library, who tracked down many of the books and helped us throughout this work.

How the Books Were Selected

"You just have to put *Benny's Bad Day* on your list. It's great. I will write you what it is about." — Jenny

We began our search by accident and in stages spanning many years. While teaching high school science, George was asked to test a new science program using students who were at least two years behind their grade level in reading. The materials arrived — six large books for each student and a selection of *Scientific American* reprints to be read by the students. There was no way that the students selected because of their poor reading skills could read this sophisticated coursework — or so we thought. The only problem was that the students did not agree. They were interested in the new program and were soon reading the magazine articles and pointing out errors in the texts.

It has been 20 years since George was approached by the University of Southern California to help train science teachers in a recruitment program for the Los Angeles City schools. That first class was a shock. Only half of the beginning teachers turned out to be interested in science. The others were eager to learn how to teach young people to read. A frantic search among reading experts finally revealed the key to reading as scholars knew it then: "Just get a book the child can read and be sure he or she reads it. Then get another book the child can read. . . ." But how could one know which books the young reader could and would read? The earlier experience of testing a science program suggested that interest was at least as important as experience with the vocabulary and sentence structure.

Some years later, we became involved in looking for good children's books to serve as bases for films. There is a common feeling, backed by some research, that young people are likely to want to read books after they have seen films based on them. Whatever the reason, this seems to be so, provided that the film is true to the characters and story in the book, particularly to the characters.

Two elements seemed to be important in selecting books for young people to read alone: The books must be based on concepts that the young reader was interested in or could be interested in. Also, the vocabulary, sentence structure, and sentence length—those elements of reading most attended to in school—would have to be within reach of the reader whose conceptual interest was touched by the book.

From those beginnings, we began examining children's books to find those with matching conceptual interest and the usual readability measures. We began our search by enlisting young readers to examine books that appeared on current lists of excellent children's books, for example, the American Library Association (ALA) Notable Children's Books and the "best books" lists of *School Library Journal.* We applied readability scales to books from these lists to sort those whose vocabulary and English range were far from the intended audience—the primary-level reader. We listened while young readers read the books to us and told us about them. Eventually, the young people began to recommend books they had discovered for themselves. Judy Cantor, head librarian at the UCLA's University Elementary School, helped us select other books to investigate. Her selection was largely based on the books that received the widest circulation in her library.

Judging readability of books is relatively easy. Several scales have been developed through many years of research that apply vocabulary knowledge, sentence structure and length, and word length for the purpose of rating the reading level of books. We used two scales to determine the range of readability for the books: the Spache Readability Formula and the Fry Readability Scale. However, we were reluctant to rely on packaged readability scales—mostly because we have become acutely aware that readability stretches or shrinks with the interest generated for the reading task. We supplemented the information given to us by applying the Spache and Fry Scales with information gathered directly from young readers. We asked them to tell us which books they could read and which books they *wanted* to read. We listened to them read aloud; and we asked them to tell us what the books were about and why they did or did not like them. Then the readers were asked to tell us what they thought about the illustrations. Some of the readers began to suggest books that we should look at. Thus *Benny's Bad Day* was added, as was *Marvin K. Mooney, Will You Please Go Now* — as were some books that interested young readers even though they are not usually thought of as primary reading books.

This compilation leans more toward books that are of most interest to young readers and less toward measures of readability. That bias came from personal experiences that suggested that children will struggle beyond the limits of their vocabulary to read something that interests them.

This text begins with those books that are intended to build the ideas of page turning and storytelling—often with no words at all. It then goes from books for the beginning to sophisticated books that third graders like to read. In the process of selection and classification, we found some "universal truths." No matter how often the theme is repeated or how silly the characters seem to become with age, young readers like to identify with old familiar characters, such as Curious George or George and Martha. We have therefore noted the books that are parts of series (see the appendix).

Another "truth" we have not totally come to grips with: There are many more books that interest girls than that interest boys—or is it that there are more girls interested in reading than boys? We do not know. But searching for good books for boys seemed to be a worthwhile challenge. One reader, Sean, gave us a list of everything he read for a year, and we used his suggestions to add more books to our list.

As we looked back at the books selected, we noted that many of them contain appealing animal characters with humanlike behavior. Young readers like to think they are mature, and thus books that appeared to be conceptually juvenile were eliminated. At the same time, these readers seem to be most interested in characters and in antics that reflect their own daily experiences. Using animals in these situations allows the young reader to examine problem situations they themselves confront without feeling awkward or self-conscious. For example, a bear burns the toast, takes a jelly sandwich to school, and winds up with the jelly all over its clean clothes. Many children have been that clumsy, but it is easier to accept and even laugh at such mistakes when a bear makes them.

ORGANIZATION

Although we applied readability scales to every book, we do not feel they are a total indication of the usefulness of the book. Thus the books have been organized to account for a wider range of abilities than is usually ascribed by readability scales, including some judgments of concept appropriateness in forming the lists. This book is organized by the half year, beginning with preword reading books. Thus, there are seven chapters in the book:

1 Books for the beginning reader
2 Books for the first half of grade one
3 Books for the second half of grade one
4 Books for the first half of grade two
5 Books for the second half of grade two
6 Books for the first half of grade three
7 Books for the second half of grade three

Wordless or nearly wordless books do not lend themselves to formal readability studies. Despite the fact that there are few or no words, the stories are not always easy to comprehend. These books cannot be simply classified as the easiest among the entries. Thus, Chapter 1 leans heavily toward ease of conceptual recognition—the reader will recognize and probably have experienced the depicted concept.

The appendix lists those selected books that are in a series. All titles in the series have been listed, even those not discussed in this volume. Following the appendix are four indexes: a Subject Index, a Readability Index, an Author Index, and a Title Index.

A few of the books selected are currently out of print or out of stock indefinitely; however, they are still available from public libraries. These books are designated in the bibliographic information with o.p. (out of print) or o.s.i. (out of stock indefinitely).

CONCEPT LEVEL

Our definition of concept level is where the reader is capable of understanding a concept within his or her realm of experience. A *desire* to understand this concept must exist. For example, a third grader understands the loss of a first tooth, but it is not on his or her concept level, since the realm of experience for this event occurred in the first grade.

The books within a chapter range from fairly simple stories such as a book about a boy and his teddy bear to a book full of details and complex pictures such as an Oriental folktale. The books with the simplest readability and concept levels are classified as *easy*. Within each grade range, the books progress from *easy*, through *average*, to *challenging*. A list of these groups begins each chapter and is followed by an annotated and alphabetical list, by author, of all the books for this reading level.

SUBJECT MATTER

Just as young people like to identify with old familiar characters, they are often attracted to subjects with which they have had past experience or which are of immediate concern in their personal lives. On a more subtle level, a pleasant reading experience with, for example, an adventure story encourages reading of more adventures. The range of genres assigned to the entries in this volume includes

Adventure	Humor
Concept book	Mystery
Fantasy	Nonfiction
Folklore	Realistic fiction
Historical fiction	

As Rebecca Lukens points out in *A Critical Handbook of Children's Literature*, picture books cross genre lines. James Stevenson has written a series of books in which the problems a brother and sister face inspire their grandfather to share some fantastic "memories" with them. The brother and sister's problems — for example, their anxiety on Halloween — suggest that the genre is realistic fiction. At the same time, since a large share of the book is devoted to Grandpa's yarns, this book has been assigned to fantasy. The genre that predominates is the one to which the title is assigned.

Picture books also call for adjustments to our accepted understanding of genres. The heroes and heroines in these stories are often animals with human qualities and problems. Amanda the pig has a big brother, Oliver, who wants to do everything she can. Like other animal stories, the feelings and problems of the humanlike characters are realistic fiction. In different stories characters try an everyday experience for the first time, and so the genre becomes adventure. The girl in Ann Jonas's *The Trek* is frightened on her walk to school by a jungle of animals that she imagines she sees. Her first trip to school is an adventure. Finally, some stories are so delightfully funny that their overriding purpose seems to be the laughter they inspire. Bernard Wiseman's character Morris is a very silly moose, and *Morris Tells Boris Mother Moose Stories and Rhymes* is clearly meant to tickle the reader's fancy. Thus, the genre *humor* is assigned to this book.

More specific than the genres are the subjects assigned to each entry. Our guide to these subjects has been the Library of Congress Subject Headings, for example, holidays and stories in rhyme. The Subject Headings were created in 1965 by the Library of Congress. This CARD program's purpose was to provide a more appropriate subject guide to children's books.

1

Books for the Beginning Reader: Wordless or Nearly Wordless Books

This chapter lists books that encourage beginning readers to turn the pages and create a story from the pictures. Some of the books encourage readers to build vocabulary by matching printed words or pictures.

EASY

Aruego, Jose and Ariane Dewey. *We Hide You Seek*
Briggs, Raymond. *The Snowman*
Burningham, John. *The Friend*
Gibbons, Gail. *Tool Book*
Gomi, Taro. *Where's the Fish?*
Hutchins, Pat. *One Hunter*
Winter, Paula. *The Bear and the Fly: A Story*

AVERAGE

Berenstain, Stan and Jan Berenstain. *Bears on Wheels*
Carle, Eric. *Do You Want to Be My Friend?*
Crews, Donald. *Freight Train*
LeSieg, Theo. *Ten Apples Up on Top!*
Winter, Paula. *Sir Andrew*
Wolcott, Patty. *Pirates, Pirates over the Salt, Salt Sea*

CHALLENGING

Ahlberg, Allan. *Help!*
Bang, Molly. *The Grey Lady and the Strawberry Snatcher*

CHALLENGING (cont.) ═══════════════════════════

Drescher, Henrik. *Simon's Book*
Florian, Douglas. *Airplane Ride*
Goodall, John S. *Paddy Pork — Odd Jobs*
Lobel, Arnold. *On Market Street*
McCully, Emily Arnold. *Picnic*
Maestro, Betsy and Giulio Maestro. *Busy Day: A Book of Action Words*
Spier, Peter. *Peter Spier's Rain*

AHLBERG, Allan. *Help!* Illus. by Colin McNaughton. Random House, 1985. ISBN: 0-394-97190-6
In this puzzlelike book, pictures with labels often in the form of equations encourage the beginning reader to recognize words and to build new ones. The illustrations are cleverly contrived to create new words from common words that can be read by association with the picture. Cars become castles in the wild imagination of Allan Ahlberg.
Genre: Concept book
Subject: Vocabulary

ARUEGO, Jose and Ariane Dewey. *We Hide You Seek.* Illus. by the authors. Greenwillow, 1979. ISBN: 0-688-80201-X
In this book the hippos are playing hide and seek. But it is hard to hide when you are small and pink. The little hippo tries to hide everywhere possible, with the reader easily following wherever it goes. Finally, the little pink hippo finds just the right place to hide. The surprise on the last page will delight the young reader who has been fooled into believing that there is really no place the little hippo can hide.
Genre: Adventure
Subject: Hippopotamuses

BANG, Molly. *The Grey Lady and the Strawberry Snatcher.* Illus. by the author. Four Winds, 1980. ISBN: 0-02-708140-0
A funny-looking bandit in a floppy purple hat is following the Grey Lady as she shops. The bandit is looking for a chance to snatch the strawberries she is carrying. Unaware of her follower, the Grey Lady moves in and out of places and crowds of people. The bandit has trouble keeping up with her, and it looks as if the

Grey Lady will be safe. But then the bandit finds a skateboard, and the chase really gets exciting. Detailed, brightly colored illustrations exaggerate the path the two characters follow. This wordless story provides beginning readers with a lively plot in pictures that encourage readers to guess what will happen next.

Genre: Adventure
Subject: Robbers and outlaws
Award: Caldecott Medal Honor Books, 1981

BERENSTAIN, Stan and Jan Berenstain. *Bears on Wheels*. Illus. by the authors. Random House, 1969. ISBN: 0-394-80967-X
This is more than a simple counting book. Though not truly a wordless book, the few words in it are frequently repeated, making it a good choice for the reader just starting out. *One* bear approaches a *uni*cycle, but the group and the kinds of vehicles change in a random fashion. Young readers must be able to count and have some idea about what the numbers represent. By taking the bears on and off the cycles, the book leads the reader into adding and subtracting. This is one of many books involving the Berenstain bears.

Genre: Concept book
Subjects: Bears; counting

BRIGGS, Raymond. *The Snowman*. Illus. by the author. Random House, 1978. ISBN: 0-394-93973-5
A boy sets out to build a snowman. However, this is not the usual snowman, for just as the boy adds the finishing touches to his sculpture, the snow figure comes to life. Together the snowman and its creator fly off to adventure. Softly colored pencil drawings tell the story clearly in a wordless book that invites the young reader to exercise imagination.

Genre: Fantasy
Subjects: Dreams; snow

BURNINGHAM, John. *The Friend*. Illus. by the author. Crowell, 1975. ISBN: 0-690-01273-X
Arthur is the best friend of the young storyteller in this book. The storyteller follows their play and squabbles in sunshine and rain. Simple, almost childlike illustrations prepare the reader to follow the few words on the opposing pages. Using just 43 words,

this story reveals that even if people are best friends they may not want to play together all the time and might even quarrel sometimes. It also shows that true best friends remain best friends through every situation.

Genre: Realistic fiction
Subject: Friendship

CARLE, Eric. *Do You Want to Be My Friend?* Illus. by the author. Crowell, 1971. ISBN: 0-690-24276-X
A very tiny mouse sets out to find a friend. Doesn't anyone want to be its friend? It asks everyone, even the animal with the big tail and whiskers. No one answers the mouse's question until the little hero finally finds the perfect friend for a mouse. The words in the title are the only words in this book, making it an easy one for the beginner who wants to "read it by myself." The simple block figures resemble brightly colored paper cutouts, adding to the feeling of an easy-to-handle story.

Genre: Adventure
Subjects: Mice; friendship; loneliness

CREWS, Donald. *Freight Train.* Illus. by the author. Greenwillow, 1978. ISBN: 0-688-80165-X
As a freight train passes through the pages of this book, the reader is introduced in pictures and words to all its different cars. The narrative names the cars and discusses the trip. Large, clear pictures of the cars show the range of shapes needed to ship supplies. The cars are brightly colored, and as a bonus a color is introduced along with the shape of each car. Young readers will enjoy relating the shapes of cars to the names and then trying to tell what kind of cargo each freight car might carry.

Genre: Concept book
Subjects: Railroads; color
Award: Caldecott Medal Honor Books, 1979

DRESCHER, Henrik. *Simon's Book.* Illus. by the author. Lothrop, 1983. ISBN: 0-688-02085-2
Simon is drawing pictures for his book, an adventure story about a dragon. When Simon draws the dragon, it comes to life and chases him. It looks as if that very awesome beast will really hurt Simon. Simon uses his paints to create all sorts of obstacles for the charging dragon, but the beast is determined to catch the

boy. The wordless story ends happily when the reader discovers why the dragon is chasing Simon. Bright splotches of color over line sketches develop a feeling of suspense as Simon tries to escape the dragon.

Genre: Fantasy
Subjects: Drawing; monsters

FLORIAN, Douglas. *Airplane Ride.* Illus. by the author. Crowell, 1984. ISBN: 0-690-04365-1
The airplane in the story is not today's typical plane. It is an old biplane that moves gracefully and slowly through the air. From the seat in the plane, the reader can see a different view of the United States as the pilot soars over mountains, cities, rivers, and plains. The story, told in pictures, gives the experience of flying to the young aviator.

Genre: Realistic fiction
Subjects: Airplanes; geography

GIBBONS, Gail. *Tool Book.* Illus. by the author. Holiday House, 1982. ISBN: 0-8234-0444-7
The names of the tools in a toolbox are the only words in this book. Each page shows a tool illustrated by a bold drawing in strong colors. Young readers can identify the tool and match it with the name as they learn about common tools. This is a good book for building self-esteem, as the reader sees tools that he or she already knows and can identify.

Genre: Nonfiction
Subject: Tools

GOMI, Taro. *Where's the Fish?* Illus. by the author. Morrow, 1977. ISBN: 0-688-06241-5
A bright red fish jumps out of its fishbowl and begins a game of hide and seek with the audience in this very easy-to-read book. The narrative asks questions that are answered by the pictures, and the next page confirms the response. Brightly colored block pictures make the game simple enough to keep the interest of a beginning reader. The errant fish is easy to identify, even when it mixes with many other red fish.

Genre: Mystery
Subjects: Fish; games

GOODALL, John S. *Paddy Pork—Odd Jobs.*   Illus. by the author. Atheneum, 1983. ISBN: 0-689-50293-1
Paddy Pork has decided to make a career of doing odd jobs. He will take on any job—wallpapering, cleaning, or whatever he's hired to do. But Paddy always has trouble. He seems to turn each job into a disaster for himself and his employer. Young readers will identify with the feeling of trying to do something new. Paddy's escapades are illustrated in small, simple, soft-colored sketches that are exaggerated to bring out the main details of the wordless story. This is one of a series of books about the adventures of Paddy Pork.

Genre: Adventure
Subject: Pigs

HUTCHINS, Pat. *One Hunter.*   Illus. by the author. Greenwillow, 1982. ISBN: 0-688-00615-9
A bungling hunter is out on a hunt. He doesn't appear to see very well. He can't even see and count the large animals that are very close to him. However, the animals see the hunter, and roles are reversed; soon the hunter is being chased. While the reader counts the animals, the plot leads to a different catch than the hunter intended.

Genre: Adventure
Subject: Counting

LeSIEG, Theo. *Ten Apples Up on Top!*   Illus. by Roy McKie. Beginner, 1961. ISBN: 0-394-80019-2
Theo LeSieg is a pen name of Theodor Geisel (Dr. Seuss), and this story makes its author readily recognizable. In this book, some of the imaginary animals carry apples on their heads. As the stack of apples grows, the animals and the readers count them. The animals have a contest to see how many apples can ride in one stack; this is fun until the lions come. The narrative is rhythmic and humorous, and fanciful pictures by Roy McKie hold to the Dr. Seuss tradition—cartoonish and bold.

Genre: Concept book
Subjects: Counting; apples

LOBEL, Arnold. *On Market Street.*   Illus. by Anita Lobel. Greenwillow, 1981. ISBN: 0-688-80309-1

This is an unusual alphabet book that takes the reader on a trip down Market Street. For each letter there is a vendor whose picture leads the beginning reader to find examples of a word. For example, *V* is for *vegetables*, and the vendor's body is made of lettuce, corn, and potatoes. The book is illustrated in bright colors with a generous amount of detail.

Genre: Concept book
Subjects: Alphabet; shopping

McCULLY, Emily Arnold. *Picnic.* Illus. by the author. Harper & Row, 1984. ISBN: 0-06-024099-7
Everyone, including the reader, is invited to a picnic. However, the reader will have to figure out what to bring and do at the picnic. In this wordless picture book all the other guests are mice. The simple line drawings tell the fanciful story in soft watercolors.

Genre: Fantasy
Subjects: Mice; picnics

MAESTRO, Betsy and Giulio Maestro. *Busy Day: A Book of Action Words.* Illus. by the authors. Crown, 1978. ISBN: 0-517-53288-3 (o.p.)
Each circus picture in this beginning word book emphasizes an activity that can be named by a single action word. The one word is the narrative for the page. The reader can decipher the word by naming the action in the illustration. Action in the circus leads to visually entertaining pictures, such as the elephant that tries to fit on the top of a bunk bed.

Genre: Concept book
Subject: Verbs

SPIER, Peter. *Peter Spier's Rain.* Illus. by the author. Doubleday, 1982. ISBN: 0-385-15484-4
In this brightly colored wordless book, Peter Spier shows all the things that Peter and his sister do to enjoy a rainy day. The book is filled with different size sketches, from small ones grouped together on a single page to one large picture that covers a two-page spread.

Genre: Realistic fiction
Subject: Rain

WINTER, Paula. *The Bear and the Fly: A Story.* Illus. by the author. Crown, 1976. ISBN: 0-517-52605-0
The three bears in this family are just sitting down to dinner when along comes a pesky fly. Papa Bear is irritated and sets out to get rid of the busy intruder. But the fly leads Papa on a wild chase before the end of the story. Boldly outlined, block-colored illustrations make it easy to follow this wordless story and anticipate what will come next. The pictures encourage beginning book handlers to use their own words.

Genre: Humor
Subjects: Families; bears; flies
Award: ALA Notable Children's Books, 1976

WINTER, Paula. *Sir Andrew.* Illus. by the author. Crown, 1980. ISBN: 0-517-53911-X
Sir Andrew is a silly donkey. It is a nice day and he plans to go for a little walk. However, he is so vain that he must get all dressed up. In his fancy clothes, the donkey has not gone far when he has an accident. Now he needs a crutch. This is only the beginning of his problems. Line drawings filled with shades of oranges and blues show all that happens in this wordless story.

Genre: Humor
Subjects: Donkeys; pride

WOLCOTT, Patty. *Pirates, Pirates over the Salt, Salt Sea.* Illus. by Bill Morrison. Addison-Wesley, 1981. ISBN: 0-201-08335-3
On an imaginary sailing voyage, the animals first meet a whale. The crew makes a friend of the whale. When their ship meets another one with a wild crew of pirates, the whale comes to their rescue. The very few words used in this story are repeated rhythmically.

Genre: Fantasy
Subject: Pirates

2

Books for the First Half of Grade One
Readability: 1.0–1.4

This chapter lists books that are appropriate both in readability and in concept for beginning first graders. The special blend of illustrations and narrative in the books helps the beginning reader decipher the story.

EASY

Asch, Frank. *Bear's Bargain*
———. *Goodnight, Horsey*
———. *Just Like Daddy*
Bang, Molly. *Ten, Nine, Eight*
Brown, Marc Tolan. *The True Francine*
Brown, Marcia. *How Hippo!*
Dr. Seuss. *The Foot Book*
———. *Marvin K. Mooney, Will You Please Go Now?*
———. *One Fish, Two Fish, Red Fish, Blue Fish*
Gray, Catherine D. and James Gray. *Tammy and the Gigantic Fish*
Hillert, Margaret. *Birthday Car*
———. *The Snow Baby*
Johnston, Tony. *Odd Jobs*
Kalan, Robert. *Jump, Frog, Jump!*
Kim, Joy. *Come on Up*
Nakatani, Chiyoko. *My Teddy Bear*
Nødset, Joan L. *Go Away, Dog*
Stadler, John. *Hooray for Snail!*
Tafuri, Nancy. *Have You Seen My Duckling?*

EASY (cont.)

Watanabe, Shigeo. *How Do I Put It On?*
———. *I Can Build a House!*
———. *I Can Ride It!*
Wood, Audrey. *The Napping House*

AVERAGE

Asch, Frank. *Sand Cake*
Berenstain, Stan and Jan Berenstain. *Inside, Outside, Upside Down*
Blos, Jean. *Martin's Hats*
Christian, Mary Blount. *Penrod's Pants*
Dr. Seuss. *Hop on Pop*
Domanska, Janina. *Little Red Hen*
Ets, Marie H. *Just Me*
Hillert, Margaret. *The Boy and the Goats*
———. *Tom Thumb*
Hoff, Syd. *Henrietta Goes to the Fair*
———. *Henrietta's Fourth of July*
Hutchins, Pat. *Rosie's Walk*
Jonas, Ann. *The Trek*
Lionni, Leo. *It's Mine*
Lopshire, Robert. *I Want to Be Somebody New*
Maris, Ron. *Are You There, Bear?*
Peppe, Rodney. *Odd One Out*
Prager, Annabelle. *The Surprise Party*
Testa, Fulvio. *If You Take a Paintbrush: A Book of Colors*
Wheeler, Cindy. *Marmalade's Nap*
———. *Marmalade's Picnic*
———. *Marmalade's Yellow Leaf*
Wolcott, Patty. *Super Sam and the Salad Garden*

CHALLENGING

Alexander, Martha. *We Never Get to Do Anything*
Alexander, Sue. *Witch, Goblin, and Ghost's Book of Things to Do*
Blocksma, Mary. *Did You Hear That?*
dePaola, Tomie. *Andy: That's My Name*
Dr. Seuss. *I Can Read with My Eyes Shut!*
Domanska, Janina. *I Saw a Ship A'Sailing*
Dunrea, Oliver. *Eddy B, Pigboy*

Gackenbach, Dick. *What's Claude Doing?*
Lobel, Anita. *The Straw Maid*
Lobel, Arnold. *Mouse Tales*
Sendak, Maurice. *Pierre*
Wiseman, Bernard. *Morris Has a Cold*
———. *Penny's Poodle Puppy, Pickle*

ALEXANDER, Martha. *We Never Get to Do Anything.* Illus. by the author. Dial, 1970. ISBN: 0-8037-9415-0
As is often the case, there is just nothing to do. Adam wants his mom to save the day by taking him swimming. When she says no, Adam is left on his own and finds a funny way to go swimming without her. Line drawings in soft colors lend an air of reality to the three characters in the story: Rufus the dog, Adam, and his mother. The illustrations are small but appealing.

Genre: Realistic fiction
Subjects: Family life; swimming

ALEXANDER, Sue. *Witch, Goblin, and Ghost's Book of Things to Do.* Illus. by Jeanette Winter. Pantheon, 1982. ISBN: 0-394-94612-X
Who would like to learn a magic trick? Or make a secret code? Does anyone want to act in a show? This is a book of things to do and games to play. The cartoonlike line drawings with color shadings show how to follow the directions.

Genre: Nonfiction
Subject: Amusements

ASCH, Frank. *Bear's Bargain.* Illus. by the author. Prentice-Hall, 1985. ISBN: 0-13-071606-5
Bear has a friend, Little Bird. They do almost everything together, but there is one thing Bear can't do—fly. Everyday he tries to convince Little Bird to teach him how to fly until finally Little Bird agrees. Bear's attempts and his payment in the bargain with Little Bird result in an entertaining story with the message that it is better just to be oneself. This is one in a series of books about Bear by Frank Asch.

Genre: Fantasy
Subjects: Animals; self-esteem

ASCH, Frank. *Goodnight, Horsey.*   Illus. by the author. Prentice-Hall, 1981. ISBN: 0-13-360461-6
Every child has played this trick to postpone bedtime. Dad is talked into just one more horse ride. This time the ride turns into a fantasy in which one of the two get tired enough to go to sleep. Illustrations made bold by solid outlines around blocks of color tell the story in pictures to help the beginning reader.

Genre: Realistic fiction
Subjects: Bedtime; family life

ASCH, Frank. *Just Like Daddy.*   Illus. by the author. Prentice-Hall, 1981. ISBN: 0-13-514042-0
The little bear does everything just the way his father does. They dress in the same fashion, eat breakfast alike, and even go out the door in the same way. But everything changes when the whole family goes fishing. The one sentence on each page and the repeated use of the title make this entertaining story easy to read. Simple, boldly colored drawings outlined in black illustrate the family's activities and their emotions. This is one in a series of books about bears by Frank Asch.

Genre: Humor
Subjects: Bears; families; fishing

ASCH, Frank. *Sand Cake.*   Illus. by the author. Parents Magazine, 1979. ISBN: 0-686-86571-5
Baby Bear quickly gets bored and hungry when the family visits the beach. He wants a piece of cake, and Papa Bear promises to cook one if Baby Bear will eat it. Papa uses his imagination to get the ingredients: flour, milk, and eggs. The cake turns out well, but it's made of sand. So how will Baby Bear eat it? He soon finds a way and ends up with a real piece of cake. This is a bear story by Frank Asch with his characteristic block-color drawings of humanlike bears. This is one in a series of books about bears by Frank Asch.

Genre: Fantasy
Subjects: Bears; cake; family life

BANG, Molly. *Ten, Nine, Eight.*   Illus. by the author. Greenwillow, 1983. ISBN: 0-688-00906-9
Ten small toes, nine soft friends — a father and a daughter play a counting game every night before going to bed. The countdown

is done in lines that rhyme. The soothing tone of the book makes this book useful as a gentle, quiet, bedtime story.

Genre: Concept book
Subjects: Bedtime; counting; stories in rhyme

BERENSTAIN, Stan and Jan Berenstain. *Inside, Outside, Upside Down.* Illus. by the authors. Random House, 1968. ISBN: 0-394-81142-9
What could be both inside and outside at the same time? It's the object on these pages, and it is also upside down. In a book about position, the Berenstains make clear the relativity of positions and at the same time reveal objects that can be described using more than one position.

Genre: Concept book
Subjects: Position; nonsense verses

BLOCKSMA, Mary. *Did You Hear That?* Illus. by Sandra C. Kalthoff. Childrens, 1983. ISBN: 0-516-01581-8
The girl in this story hears a noise in the night and imagines that all kinds of strange creatures are lurking under her bed. Each new creature adds to the fantasy until the bedroom is bulging with strange beings.

Genre: Fantasy
Subject: Fear

BLOS, Jean. *Martin's Hats.* Illus. by Marc Simont. Morrow, 1984. ISBN: 0-688-02027-5
Martin likes to play with hats. For example, when he puts on an explorer's hat, he becomes an explorer; a cowboy hat changes him into a cowboy. One by one, Martin tries on the hats and imagines he is the character. Finally, one hat is left, and that hat makes Martin feel just like himself.

Genre: Realistic fiction
Subjects: Boys; hats; imagination

BROWN, Marc Tolan. *The True Francine.* Illus. by the author. Little, Brown, 1981. ISBN: 0-316-11212-7
Francine and Muffy are such good friends that when Muffy is caught cheating on a test, Francine takes the blame. When this is fine by Muffy, trouble starts between the two friends. Brightly colored cartoonlike drawings illustrate the characters, includ-

ing monkeys and other animals, as well as Francine, Muffy, and Mr. Ratburn, the teacher.

Genre: Realistic fiction
Subjects: Honesty; friendship; animals

BROWN, Marcia. *How Hippo!* Illus. by the author. Scribner, 1969. ISBN: 0-684-12543-9 (o.s.i.)
The baby hippo is having a wonderful time. It hasn't strayed far from its mother, but Mom thinks the baby is lost. The antics of the carefree baby and the worries of the mother fill this story. The soft-colored woodcuts, slightly exaggerated drawings, keep readers informed about both the baby and the mother.

Genre: Adventure
Subjects: Families; hippopotamuses

CHRISTIAN, Mary Blount. *Penrod's Pants.* Illus. by Jane Dyer. Macmillan, 1986. ISBN: 0-02-718520-6
Five stories about Penrod the Porcupine and Griswold the Bear tell about the adventures of these two friends. Penrod gets a pair of pants as a present and wears out Griswold as they shop to find another pair exactly like the gift — including grandma's five dollars in the pocket. Then Griswold gets an "almost" perfect pair of pants that become perfect when Penrod fixes them — perfect for Penrod. In each adventure, Penrod unwittingly ends up a winner.

Genre: Adventure
Subjects: Bears; porcupines; friendship

dePAOLA, Tomie. *Andy: That's My Name.* Illus. by the author. Prentice-Hall, 1973. ISBN: 0-13-036731-1
In this fun-with-words book, Andy has a load of letters that he shows off by using them to spell his name. Then Andy and his friends arrange, add to, and rearrange letters to build other words. This book has solid outlines around soft pinks, yellows, browns, and oranges; the cartoonlike figures draw readers into the word game.

Genre: Concept book
Subject: Words

DR. SEUSS. *The Foot Book.* Illus. by the author. Random House, 1968. ISBN: 0-394-90937-2

Left foot, right foot, big foot, small foot, trick foot, sick foot—a foot seeker encounters every kind of foot imaginable in this rhyming and counting book. The simple, bold, cartoonlike drawings are filled with imaginary animals and people.

Genre: Concept book
Subject: Feet

DR. SEUSS. *Hop on Pop.* Illus. by the author. Beginner, 1963. ISBN: 0-394-90029-4
The animals in this story play all day and fight all night. They play games in which everyone can participate, their favorite one being hop on pop. Bright, solid colors fill the cartoonlike pictures that illustrate the rhyming story of a family with a favorite pastime.

Genre: Humor
Subject: Amusements

DR. SEUSS. *I Can Read with My Eyes Shut!* Illus. by the author. Random House, 1978. ISBN 0-394-93912-3
The Cat in the Hat is a central character in this book about the pleasures of reading and observing. In the rhyming narrative of Dr. Seuss, young readers are led to see that while many things can be imagined and dreamed, much more can be seen and enjoyed if they keep their eyes open. This is one in a series of books about the Cat in the Hat.

Genre: Fantasy
Subjects: Reading; observing

DR. SEUSS. *Marvin K. Mooney, Will You Please Go Now?* Illus. by the author. Random House, 1972. ISBN: 0-394-92490-8
This book is easier to read than the words at first suggest. Rhyme and comical pictures illustrate the most difficult words—all of them noises—making this book an almost certain success for the beginning reaader. The theme—there is really no story—is easy to understand. Someone wants Marvin to go *now* and doesn't care how.

Genre: Concept book
Subject: Language

DR. SEUSS. *One Fish, Two Fish, Red Fish, Blue Fish.* Illus. by the author. Random House, 1960. ISBN: 0-394-80013-3

The fish in this book are everywhere. Some are high and some are low, and one fish, named Clark, is even in the dark. The fanciful fish bring out concepts of color, counting, and position. Dr. Seuss uses solid, bright colors in cartoonlike characters typical of his imaginative style.

Genre: Concept book
Subjects: Color; counting; position

DOMANSKA, Janina. *I Saw a Ship A'Sailing.* Illus. by the author. Macmillan, 1972. ISBN: 0-02-732940-0 (o.s.i.)
What a great sailing ship! It has silk sails and golden masts and is filled with tasty things to eat. But there is a very strange crew on board. Fanciful pen-and-ink illustrations create the wonder of sky and crew in this traditional Mother Goose rhyme.

Genre: Folklore and fairy tales
Subject: Ships

DOMANSKA, Janina. *Little Red Hen.* Illus. by the author. Macmillan, 1973. ISBN: 0-02-732820-1 (o.s.i.)
In a retelling of an old tale, the Little Red Hen begins to grind corn and make some bread. No one wants to help with the work, but everyone wants to share in the eating when the bread is finally finished. This folktale is illustrated with drawings made from combinations of geometric shapes, boldly outlined and brightly colored with solid hues.

Genre: Folklore and fairy tales
Subjects: Work; sharing

DUNREA, Oliver. *Eddy B, Pigboy.* Illus. by the author. Macmillan, 1983. ISBN: 0-689-50277-X
Eddy B lives on a farm. His job is to watch the pigs and bring them into the sty at the end of the day. The mother pig is so big that Eddy needs to think of a trick in order to get her and the piglets home safely. Small realistic drawings illustrate the sure way that Eddy B accomplishes his task.

Genre: Realistic fiction
Subjects: Farms; pigs

ETS, Marie H. *Just Me.* Illus. by the author. Viking, 1965. ISBN: 0-670-41109-4
Occasionally it's fun to imagine you are something else. The girl in this story pretends to be a horse, a dragon, and a robot. She

enjoys herself so much that she forgets what is real. So her family brings her back to reality by helping her act and even eat like a horse.

Genre: Realistic fiction
Subject: Families
Award: Caldecott Medal Honor Books, 1966

GACKENBACH, Dick. *What's Claude Doing?* Illus. by the author. Clarion, 1984. ISBN: 0-89919-224-6
Claude, the big friendly dog, usually comes to meet the school bus. He also goes ice skating with the children, and he loves to chase cats. But today Claude won't leave home. He won't even come out when his friends call, and they wonder what the dog could be doing. In the end there is a very good reason for Claude's staying home.

Genre: Realistic fiction
Subjects: Dogs; friendship

GRAY, Catherine D. and James Gray. *Tammy and the Gigantic Fish.* Illus. by William Joyce. Harper & Row, 1983. ISBN: 0-06-022138-0
When Father and Grandfather decide to go fishing, Tammy goes along. Both Grandpa and Dad catch fish, but Tammy just catches crawdads. Finally, it is time to go home. Just as they are leaving, Tammy catches the biggest fish of the day. The fish is so big that it won't fit in the car, but Tammy manages to solve the problem. Small pen-and-ink drawings capture the sadness of the big fish and Tammy's dilemma as she decides what to do with it.

Genre: Realistic fiction
Subjects: Fishing; family life

HILLERT, Margaret. *Birthday Car.* Illus. by Kelly Oechsli. Follett, 1966. ISBN: 0-695-80801-X
It is a boy's birthday, and what a great present he gets! In the back of Dad's pickup truck, there is a bright red car big enough to sit in. Now the boy can pretend to travel anywhere his imagination will take him. Readers can easily identify with the boy and his experience.

Genre: Realistic fiction
Subjects: Birthdays; family life

HILLERT, Margaret. *The Boy and the Goats.* Illus. by Yoshi Miyake. Follett, 1982. ISBN: 0-88153-004-2
A young boy has the job of tending some frisky goats. However, the garden on the other side of the fence is very attractive, and the goats jump the fence and won't come out. The boy gets help from everyone — a fox, a wolf, a rabbit, and a bee — but only one of them succeeds. The characters are outlined in bold colors and lighter shades fill in the simple figures.

Genre: Realistic fiction
Subjects: Boys; goats

HILLERT, Margaret. *The Snow Baby.* Illus. by Liz Dauber. Follett, 1969. ISBN: 0-8136-5065-8
It is snowing outside and the children are eager to go out to play, but one of them has lost her red boot. Once the boot is found, the snow play begins, with snowmen and snow castles. While exploring in the snow, the children discover a little white kitten hidden under a bush. They take it home, where their mother decides that it will make a lovely pet for the family.

Genre: Realistic fiction
Subjects: Seasons (winter); pets

HILLERT, Margaret. *Tom Thumb.* Illus. by Dennis Hockerman. Follett, 1982. ISBN: 0-695-41542-5
Tom is a very small boy. He is so small that a bird can pick him up and fly away with him. Many advantages of being small are shown, such as being able to ride on a mouse. However, as Tom's adventures unfold, the reader sees that there are formidable obstacles to being small.

Genre: Folklore and fairy tales
Subject: Folklore (Germany)

HOFF, Syd. *Henrietta Goes to the Fair.* Illus. by the author. Garrard, 1979. ISBN: 0-8116-4406-5
The farmer has a prizewinning pig of which he is very proud. He also has a very ordinary chicken named Henrietta. The pig is the farmer's entry into the competition at the county fair. When things go wrong and the pig can't compete, Henrietta comes to

the rescue and saves the farmer from a disastrous day. This is one in a series of books about Henrietta.

Genre: Adventure
Subject: Animals

HOFF, Syd. *Henrietta's Fourth of July.* Illus. by the author. Garrard, 1981. ISBN: 0-8116-4422-7
It is the Fourth of July and the farmer plans to march in the parade. Henrietta thinks this would be fun and wants to march, too. In fact, Henrietta begins to practice — left, right, left, right — just like her owner. The farmer is impressed and decides that Henrietta can march in the parade, but now all the other animals want to march with her. The farmer agrees and Henrietta trains all the animals. On the Fourth of July, the chicken carries the flag, Winthrop the pig plays the fife, and Patrick the goat plays the drums to begin a day that starts with the parade and ends with a picnic and fireworks. This is one in a series of books about Henrietta.

Genre: Fantasy
Subjects: Chickens; holidays (Fourth of July)

HUTCHINS, Pat. *Rosie's Walk.* Illus. by the author. Macmillan, 1968. ISBN: 0-02-745850-4
Rosie, a little hen, goes for a walk. Seeing her all alone, a fox imagines a fine dinner and begins to stalk Rosie. The hen doesn't know she's being followed, but her explorations lead the fox into misery. Bright, detailed pictures illustrate the story.

Genre: Adventure
Subjects: Chickens; foxes
Award: ALA Children's Notable Books, 1968

JOHNSTON, Tony. *Odd Jobs.* Illus. by the author. Putnam, 1977. ISBN: 0-399-61204-1
Odd Jobs is the name the boy goes by and it is also his trade. No job is too big or too small for Odd Jobs. At least no job is too big until he is hired to bathe a dog that turns out to be much larger than the boy could imagine.

Genre: Realistic fiction
Subject: Work

JONAS, Ann. *The Trek.*   Illus. by the author. Greenwillow, 1985.
ISBN: 0-688-04799-8
Walking to school by herself gives a girl a chance to see all kinds
of animals. The short walk is frightening, but everything turns
out fine after she finds a friend to finish the trip with her. The
art is suggestive and detailed, with the pictures hinting at the
wild animals that are shown at the end of the book. For example,
a stone walkway looks like an alligator and a hedge like a gorilla.
Genre: Adventure
Subjects: Imagination; jungle; deserts

KALAN, Robert. *Jump, Frog, Jump!*   Illus. by Byron Barton.
Greenwillow, 1981. ISBN: 0-688-80271-0
In just a few rhyming words, Kalan tells a story of adventure for
very young readers. Everything seems to be out to catch the
small frog. It is chased by a big fish, a snake, a turtle, and even
some boys who want to play. However, the frog has one advan-
tage. It can jump, and that makes the chase exciting.
Genre: Adventure
Subjects: Frogs; stories in rhyme

KIM, Joy. *Come on Up.*   Illus. by Paul Harvey. Troll, 1981. ISBN:
0-89375-511-7
A big cat easily climbs a tree, as most cats can. Then it invites
all its animal friends to "come on up." Some friends, like the
bird, manage easily, but the little cat has trouble. The little cat
can't climb that high at first, but everything changes when the
big dog comes along.
Genre: Realistic fiction
Subjects: Cats; pets

LIONNI, Leo. *It's Mine.*   Illus. by the author. Knopf, 1986. ISBN:
0-394-87000-X
Three big frogs live in a pond that contains a small island. Each
of the frogs claims a particular spot. One claims to own the island, another the water, and the third the shore. Each defends its
territory fervently and wants no interference from the others.
Then a storm strikes the pond and wreaks such havoc that all
three frogs are in danger. In the end, they find it is better to work
together than to stick selfishly to their own claims.
Genre: Adventure
Subjects: Frogs; selfishness

LOBEL, Anita. *The Straw Maid.* Illus. by the author. Greenwillow, 1983. ISBN: 0-688-00344-3
A farm girl sets out to sell the family cow to get food for her parents. On the way, she is kidnapped by three robbers and the cow runs away. The girl, though, is not easily frightened. She soon finds a way to outwit the robbers and retrieve the cow. In shades and blends of yellows and reds, the comical, simply drawn illustrations act as solid clues to the words for beginning readers.
Genre: Adventure
Subjects: Kidnapping; robbers and outlaws

LOBEL, Arnold. *Mouse Tales.* Illus. by the author. Harper & Row, 1972. ISBN: 0-06-023941-7
Papa Mouse promises to tell one mouse story to each of his seven sons—if they will go straight to bed afterward. There are seven stories in the book—tales about making a wishing well happy, seeing pictures in clouds, and even taking a bath. Each of the stories is short enough to be read in a single sitting. Small, amusing pictures illustrate the action on every page.
Genre: Realistic fiction
Subjects: Mice; short stories

LOPSHIRE, Robert. *I Want to Be Somebody New.* Illus. by the author. Beginner, 1986. ISBN: 0-394-80017-6
The same large, spotted animal that stars in *Put Me in the Zoo* has been a success in the circus. But now it wants to be something different. It used to use magic to change spots from color to color and place to place. Now it uses the same magic to change into an elephant too big to sit in a chair and into such shapes as a very small mouse with very big ears. The simple drawings with their bold spots of color help readers understand that it is best to be one's self.
Genre: Fantasy
Subjects: Animals; self-esteem

MARIS, Ron. *Are You There, Bear?* Illus. by the author. Greenwillow, 1984. ISBN: 0-688-03997-9
This story opens in a dark room full of children's toys. Someone is looking for Bear. Soon the donkey and Raggedy Ann are helping in the search. They look everywhere and finally find Bear

doing . . . just what the reader is doing. There are six or seven difficult words for beginning readers, but nearly all are made easy by pictures that are designed to help a beginner decipher the words. Dark illustrations portray the room at night and are interrupted by a circular spot with color. It's as if that part of the room is illuminated by a flashlight.

Genre: Fantasy

Subject: Toys

NAKATANI, Chiyoko. *My Teddy Bear.*   Illus. by the author. Crowell, 1976. ISBN: 0-690-01076-1 (o.p.)
A boy's best friend is his teddy bear. They do everything together. Teddy even takes a bath just like the boy. Soft watercolor drawings show the boy's fondness for his toy.

Genre: Fantasy

Subject: Toys

NØDSET, Joan L. *Go Away, Dog.*   Illus. by Crosby Bonsall. Harper & Row, 1963. ISBN: 0-06-024556-5
The boy does not like dogs. But one day he meets a dog who likes him and will not leave him alone. The story tells all the things the boy does to get rid of the dog and how the whole situation changes. The boy's feelings and the dog's are captured in black-and-white drawings colored in places with bright orange spots.

Genre: Realistic fiction

Subjects: Dogs; pets

PEPPE, Rodney. *Odd One Out.*   Illus. by the author. Viking, 1985. ISBN: 0-670-52029-2
Every picture in this book is a puzzle in which something is wrong. The job of the reader is to find the error—for example, a traffic light is in the garden and a monkey is at a school desk. The pictures are full of brightly colored figures and objects in scenes that give readers plenty to see.

Genre: Fantasy

Subject: Puzzles

PRAGER, Annabelle. *The Surprise Party.*   Illus. by Tomie dePaola. Pantheon, 1977. ISBN: 0-394-83235-8

Albert wants to have a surprise party for himself, and so he plans the whole event. The guests have arrived and everything is ready. It is such a great surprise party that even Albert is surprised by what happens.

Genre: Realistic fiction
Subjects: Parties; boys

SENDAK, Maurice. *Pierre.* Illus. by the author. Harper & Row, 1962. ISBN: 0-06-025965-5
"I don't care," says Pierre. He doesn't care about anything. He doesn't even care if his parents go out and leave him alone. But then something happens to make Pierre care very much. Bright yellow and blue pictures illustrate the story in distinctive Sendak style.

Genre: Fantasy
Subjects: Family life; lions; caring

STADLER, John. *Hooray for Snail!* Illus. by the author. Crowell, 1984. ISBN: 0-690-04412-7
The animals are playing baseball and Snail comes to bat at a critical moment in the game. The other team is delighted, but his own team and the fans are unhappy that it's slow Snail's turn at bat. In the end Snail surprises everyone with his game-winning act.

Genre: Fantasy
Subject: Snails

TAFURI, Nancy. *Have You Seen My Duckling?* Illus. by the author. Greenwillow, 1984. ISBN: 0-688-02797-0
The mother duck has too many ducklings to watch. One of them wanders away, so the mother asks everyone where it is. Only the reader can help find the missing duckling. Line drawings filled with solid colors keep the reader informed about the escapades of the lost duckling. The book is almost wordless, the words being limited to those in the title. It is an easy book for the do-it-myself beginning reader.

Genre: Adventure
Subject: Ducks
Award: Caldecott Medal Honor Books, 1985

TESTA, Fulvio. *If You Take a Paintbrush: A Book of Colors.*
Illus. by the author. Dial, 1982. ISBN: 0-8037-3829-3
Beginning with yellow, the color of the sun, the illustrations in
this book depict many colors using everyday objects. Along the
way, readers learn how to combine some colors to get others.
Full pages illustrate the color that is described in one- or two-
sentence narrations that appear boldly on pages opposite the
pictures. This introduction to colors and to mixing colors is told
in just over 100 words.

Genre: Concept book
Subject: Color

WATANABE, Shigeo. *How Do I Put It On?* Illus. by Yasuo
Ohtomo. Philomel, 1980. ISBN: 0-399-20761-9
Bear is beginning to learn to put on his clothes. However, he
doesn't do it very well. He puts pants on his head and shoes on
his ears. Everything goes wrong in the story, to the delight of
young readers who also bungle first tries at grown-up tasks. The
line drawings are filled with soft colors and a generous amount
of white space, making this book easy to handle for the beginning reader. This is one in a series of books about bears.

Genre: Concept book
Subjects: Dressing; self-esteem

WATANABE, Shigeo. *I Can Build a House!* Illus. by Yasuo
Ohtomo. Philomel, 1983. ISBN: 0-399-20950-6
A very large bear cub tries to build a house of pillows and blocks.
The bear is so big and awkward that it fails, but then tries another method to build the house. As with the other books in this
series about this bear, the story shows the young reader that trying is good and making mistakes is okay.

Genre: Concept book
Subject: Self-esteem

WATANABE, Shigeo. *I Can Ride It!* Illus. by Yasuo Ohtomo.
Philomel, 1981. ISBN: 0-399-20867-4
A very large bear cub gets on a small tricycle. After riding the
tricycle, the cub graduates to a bicycle, then to skates, and finally tries a skateboard. The cub can ride all these vehicles—
almost. This is a book about setting goals. It is illustrated with

soft, cheerful pictures that invite young readers to challenge themselves by trying something new. One large picture for each two-page spread makes the art easy to follow. This is one of a series about a bear cub who tries things for the first time.

Genre: Concept book
Subjects: Goal setting; self-esteem

WHEELER, Cindy. *Marmalade's Nap.* Illus. by the author. Knopf, 1983. ISBN: 0-394-85022-X
Marmalade the cat really needs a nap. But all the other young animals make so much noise that Marmalade can't get to sleep. Finally, the cat finds the one place that is sure to be quiet. This is one in a series of books about Marmalade.

Genre: Adventure
Subject: Cats

WHEELER, Cindy. *Marmalade's Picnic.* Illus. by the author. Knopf, 1983. ISBN: 0-394-85023-8
Marmalade the cat and a girl set out on a picnic, taking a big lunch in a picnic basket. It is a lovely day to sit in the shade and read, and that is what the girl does. Marmalade can't read, though, so the cat is left alone to explore the picnic basket and get into all sorts of mischief. Simple line drawings in soft shades of color make the story easy for readers to interpret. This is one in a series of books about Marmalade.

Genre: Adventure
Subject: Cats

WHEELER, Cindy. *Marmalade's Yellow Leaf.* Illus. by the author. Knopf, 1982. ISBN: 0-394-85024-6
Marmalade the cat watches a yellow leaf falling to the ground and being tossed by the wind. When something small and bright is moving, it must be a toy for the cat to catch. Chasing the leaf leads Marmalade into a world of fall colors and adventure. This is one in a series of books about Marmalade.

Genre: Adventure
Subject: Cats

WISEMAN, Bernard. *Morris Has a Cold.* Illus. by the author. Dodd, Mead, 1978. ISBN: 0-396-07522-3

Morris the Moose feels sick and Boris the Bear is trying to help. But Morris doesn't seem to understand. He thinks he should drop the pill Boris gives him because it is a cough drop. Anyway, what good is a cough drop when all Morris has is a "walking" nose? In simple line drawings, the characters are shown with comical facial expressions that complement the humorous tale. This is one in a series of stories about Morris the Moose and the friend he irritates, Boris the Bear.

Genre: Humor

Subjects: Friendship; animals

WISEMAN, Bernard. *Penny's Poodle Puppy, Pickle.* Illus. by the author. Garrard, 1980. ISBN: 0-8116-6080-X
On a picnic, Penny loses her poodle, Pickle. Everyone in the group is confused when Penny begins to search for the dog. Some of them even offer her a pickle.

Genre: Realistic fiction

Subjects: Dogs; words

WOLCOTT, Patty. *Super Sam and the Salad Garden.* Illus. by Marc Tolan Brown. Harper & Row, 1975. ISBN: 0-201-14253-8
A boy plants a garden of vegetables, thinking they will make a great salad. But a mean gang tears up the garden just when it is starting to grow. Now the boy is faced with the dilemma of whether to plant again. With the help of his wise dog, Sam, the boy solves the problem.

Genre: Realistic fiction

Subjects: Dogs; bullies

WOOD, Audrey. *The Napping House.* Illus. by Don Wood. Harcourt, 1984. ISBN: 0-15-256708-9
It's time for naps. Dog, cat, and all the people in the house are trying to sleep. The one thing that has no interest in napping is a small, buzzing flea. The flea nips just one of the sleepers, but that involves everyone in a chain reaction that creates trouble throughout the book.

Genre: Adventure

Subjects: Animals; sleep

3

Books for the Second Half of Grade One
Readability: 1.5–1.9

There seems to be a very limited number of books that are at this vocabulary level and still attractive to the more sophisticated, television-oriented first grader of the 1980s.

EASY

Alexander, Martha. *Maybe a Monster*
Aliki. *We Are Best Friends*
Bonsall, Crosby. *Mine's the Best*
Bulla, Clyde. *Keep Running, Allen!*
Christelow, Eileen. *Henry and the Dragon*
Crews, Donald. *Harbor*
Dabcovich, Lydia. *Sleepy Bear*
Hutchins, Pat. *The Wind Blew*
Jonas, Ann. *Two Bear Cubs*
Kantrowitz, Mildred. *Willy Bear*
Lopshire, Robert. *Put Me in the Zoo*
McPhail, David. *Emma's Pet*
———. *Great Cat*
Marshall, James. *The Guest*
Parker, Nancy Winslow. *Poofy Loves Company*
Platt, Kin. *Big Max in the Mystery of the Missing Moose*
Raskin, Ellen. *And It Rained*
Rey, H. A. *Curious George*
Rey, Margaret and H. A. Rey. *Curious George Flies a Kite*
Rylant, Cynthia. *Henry and Mudge: The First Book of Their Adventures*

EASY (cont.)

Spier, Peter. *Bored, Nothing to Do*
Stevenson, James. *Fast Friends*
Thaler, Mike. *Owly*
Wells, Rosemary. *A Lion for Lewis*
———. *Max's First Word*
Wiseman, Bernard. *Hooray for Patsy's Oink!*
———. *Morris Goes to School*
———. *Morris Tells Boris Mother Moose Stories and Rhymes*

AVERAGE

Alexander, Sue. *World Famous Muriel*
Bate, Lucy. *Little Rabbit's Loose Tooth*
Brandenberg, Franz. *Leo and Emily*
———. *Leo and Emily and the Dragon*
Browne, Anthony. *Bear Hunt*
Bulla, Clyde. *Daniel's Duck*
Carle, Eric. *The Very Busy Spider*
———. *The Very Hungry Caterpillar*
Cohen, Miriam. *Jim's Dog Muffins*
Dr. Seuss. *The Cat in the Hat*
———. *The Cat in the Hat Comes Back*
Hoban, Lillian. *Arthur's Christmas Cookies*
———. *Arthur's Funny Money*
———. *Arthur's Halloween Costume*
Hoff, Syd. *Barkley*
Isadora, Rachel. *Max*
Johnston, Tony. *Farmer Mack Measures His Pig*
Keats, Ezra Jack. *A Letter to Amy*
———. *Regards to the Man in the Moon*
Kraus, Robert. *Whose Mouse Are You?*
LeSieg, Theo. *The Tooth Book*
Lewis, Thomas P. *Mr. Sniff and the Motel Mystery*
Lexau, Joan. *The Rooftop Mystery*
Lobel, Arnold. *Owl at Home*
———. *Small Pig*
Marshall, Edward. *Fox and His Friends*
———. *Fox on Wheels*
———. *Three by the Sea*
Modell, Frank. *One Zillion Valentines*
Oxenbury, Helen. *The Dancing Class*

Pomerantz, Charlotte. *The Piggy in the Puddle*
Schatell, Brian. *Sam's No Dummy, Farmer Goff*
Sharmat, Marjorie Weinman. *Burton and Dudley*
———. *Nate the Great and the Sticky Case*
Stevenson, James. *Howard*
———. *Monty*
Thayer, Jane. *Popcorn Dragon*
Vincent, Gabrielle. *Bravo, Ernest and Celestine!*
———. *Ernest and Celestine*
———. *Merry Christmas, Ernest and Celestine*
———. *Smile, Ernest and Celestine*
Wolcott, Patty. *Pickle, Pickle, Pickle Juice*

CHALLENGING

Bang, Molly. *Tye Mae and the Magic Brush*
Brandenberg, Franz. *Everyone Ready?*
Cohen, Miriam. *Tough Jim*
Delton, Judy. *I'm Telling You Now*
Ehrlich, Amy. *Leo, Zack, and Emmie*
Lobel, Arnold. *Days with Frog and Toad*
———. *Ming Lo Moves the Mountain*
———. *Uncle Elephant*
Lund, Doris. *You Ought to See Herbert's House*
Marshall, James. *George and Martha, Back in Town*
———. *George and Martha One Fine Day*
Parish, Peggy. *Dinosaur Time*
Ricciuti, Edward R. *Donald and the Fish That Walked*
Rice, Eve. *Papa's Lemonade and Other Stories*
Stevenson, James. *That Dreadful Day*
———. *That Terrible Halloween Night*
Van Leeuwen, Jean. *Amanda Pig and Her Big Brother Oliver*
Van Woerkom, Dorothy. *Harry and Shelburt*
Waber, Bernard. *Ira Sleeps Over*
Yolen, Jane. *Mice on Ice*

ALEXANDER, Martha. *Maybe a Monster.* Illus. by the author.
Dial, 1968. ISBN: 0-8037-5508-2
The boy in the story is building a trap. While he builds, he imagines what types of animals his trap will hold and what to do with them. His dreams are filled with different animals and all

kinds of tricks. Finally, he imagines there is a monster in his trap and that he must find a way to deal with the angry beast.

Genre: Fantasy
Subjects: Monsters; fear

ALEXANDER, Sue. *World Famous Muriel.*   Illus. by Chris L. Demarest. Little, Brown, 1983. ISBN: 0-316-03131-3
Muriel is most famous as a detective, but she is also a tightrope walker. She is invited to perform her tightrope act at the Queen's birthday party, but someone takes the party decorations. Without the decorations there will be no party and Muriel will lose her once-in-a-lifetime opportunity to show off. The decorations must be found, and Muriel is the one to look for them. She can solve anything as long as there is enough of her favorite thinking food, peanut-butter cookies, and some have been prepared for the party.

Genre: Mystery
Subjects: Girls; birthdays; detective

ALIKI. *We Are Best Friends.*   Illus. by the author. Greenwillow, 1982. ISBN: 0-688-00823-2
Robert is sad because his best friend has moved away. He feels as if he will never have friends again. The situation changes when Will moves into the neighborhood, but Robert doesn't forget his first friend. Readers who have lost a friend for any reason can identify with Robert in the struggle to overcome personal sorrow.

Genre: Realistic fiction
Subject: Friendship

BANG, Molly. *Tye Mae and the Magic Brush.*   Illus. by the author. Greenwillow, 1981. ISBN: 0-688-80290-7
In this re-creation of a Chinese folktale, Tye Mae is a young painter who one day awakens to find that someone has left her a new paintbrush. It is a special brush with a golden handle. She hastens to test the brush by painting a picture of a horse. Painted by the magic brush, the horse springs to life and grows big enough to carry Tye Mae to new adventures. The soft pencil sketches are touched by spots of bright red that appear mostly in the girl's jacket.

Genre: Folklore and fairy tales
Subjects: Painting; magic; China; orphans

BATE, Lucy. *Little Rabbit's Loose Tooth.* Illus. by Diane de Groat. Crown, 1975. ISBN: 0-517-52240-3
Little Rabbit's tooth is loose enough to fall out. What should the rabbit do once it does fall out? Little Rabbit has heard of the tooth fairy but is not sure that the story is true. After exploring other things to do with the tooth, he finally decides to trust the tooth fairy. Little Rabbit knows how to ensure that the fairy will leave a gift in exchange for the tooth.

Genre: Realistic fiction
Subjects: Rabbits; teeth
Award: California Young Reader Medal, 1978

BONSALL, Crosby. *Mine's the Best.* Illus. by the author. Harper & Row, 1973. ISBN: 0-06-020578-4
A group of young friends go to the beach. Two boys have inflatable beach toys. They blow up the toys to an enormous size and then quarrel over which toy is the best. The quarrel ends in a fight in which both toys are broken. Now a girl has the best toy at the beach. This story shows how foolish it is to fight.

Genre: Realistic fiction
Subjects: Competition; boys

BRANDENBERG, Franz. *Everyone Ready?* Illus. by Aliki. Greenwillow, 1979. ISBN: 0-688-80198-6
The entire mouse family is planning a trip to visit Uncle Alfred, but they are having a difficult time getting ready to go. Finally, they get to the train station. The children manage to get on the train, but their parents are left at the station. Now the children worry that they or their parents will be lost forever, but Uncle Alfred brings the whole family together again. This book is illustrated with small cartoonlike sketches in green and pink watercolors. This is one in a series of books about the mouse family.

Genre: Adventure
Subjects: Mice; families

BRANDENBERG, Franz. *Leo and Emily.* Illus. by Aliki. Greenwillow, 1981. ISBN: 0-688-80292-3
Emily and Leo get dressed in the dark by themselves. The way the two look is enough to make their families laugh. The story follows the two friends from this escapade to a magic show. Sketchy cartoonlike drawings in shades of reds and greens help

readers identify with Leo and Emily. This is one in a series of books about the adventures of these two friends.

Genre: Realistic fiction
Subjects: Magic; friendship

BRANDENBERG, Franz. *Leo and Emily and the Dragon.*   Illus. by Aliki. Greenwillow, 1984. ISBN: 0-688-02531-5
In the first of the two stories in this book, Leo and Emily plan a dragon hunt. They are so loaded down that they seem to have taken everything with them, but they forget one important item for the trip. In the second story, Leo and Emily plan to tease a new baby-sitter. But this baby-sitter is wise; no one plays tricks on him. This is one in a series of books about the escapades of these two friends.

Genre: Realistic fiction
Subject: Friendship

BROWNE, Anthony. *Bear Hunt.*   Illus. by the author. Atheneum, 1972. ISBN: 0-698-30733-0 (o.p.)
In its bright polka-dot tie, the bear is easy to see as it experiments with many things. Its efforts lead to troubles, but this doesn't worry the bear who uses a pencil to escape from almost any situation. The illustrations are simply drawn in bright colors with ample white space, making this an inviting book for the beginning reader.

Genre: Fantasy
Subjects: Bears; hunting

BULLA, Clyde. *Daniel's Duck.*   Illus. by Joan Sandin. Harper & Row, 1979. ISBN: 0-06-444031-1
Daniel wants to carve a duck. He works very hard at the task and finally produces a fine-looking duck, except that its head is on backward. Everyone laughs at the duck. In the end Daniel realizes that his carving is both funny and original. He gains an appreciation for the unusual looking duck and for his own unique talent.

Genre: Realistic fiction
Subjects: Self-esteem; woodcarving

BULLA, Clyde. *Keep Running, Allen!* Illus. by Satomi Ichikawa. Crowell, 1978. ISBN: 0-690-01374-4

Allen is smaller than the rest of his siblings who are hiking through a field. They move very fast and tell Allen to keep running. But it's not easy for the small boy to keep up, so Allen finds a way for everyone to do things at his speed. The soft watercolors illustrate a problem common to many small children.

Genre: Realistic fiction
Subject: Brothers and sisters

CARLE, Eric. *The Very Busy Spider.* Illus. by the author. Philomel, 1984. ISBN: 0-399-21166-7

All through the day the little spider is so busy building a web that she can't even answer friends who invite her to join in their activities. In fact, the spider is so involved that she doesn't notice anything until a fly comes. But by that time the web is complete and the fly makes a fine dinner for the hardworking spider. Extra thick paper makes page turning easy, and raised lines in the pictures allow readers to feel the spider's progress with the construction of the web.

Genre: Realistic fiction
Subject: Spiders

CARLE, Eric. *The Very Hungry Caterpillar.* Illus. by the author. Philomel, 1982. ISBN: 0-529-00776-2

It all starts with a tiny egg that changes to a tiny caterpillar. The caterpillar just eats and grows. It eats so much that it gets a stomachache. As the caterpillar gets bigger, it builds a house to live in. What comes out of the house is no longer a caterpillar but a beautiful butterfly. Young readers especially enjoy the middle pages of this book, which vary in size and have holes where the hungry caterpillar has eaten his way through apples, pears, plums, and strawberries.

Genre: Realistic fiction
Subjects: Butterflies; caterpillars

CHRISTELOW, Eileen. *Henry and the Dragon.* Illus. by the author. Clarion, 1984. ISBN: 0-89919-220-3

Henry the rabbit has a problem. It is dark and time for bed. The lights are out, but something is moving in his room. A faint shadow on the wall becomes a frightening dragon that returns every night until Henry finds a way to get rid of it for good.

Genre: Realistic fiction
Subjects: Rabbits; night; fear

COHEN, Miriam. *Jim's Dog Muffins.*   Illus. by Lillian Hoban. Greenwillow, 1984. ISBN: 0-688-02565-X
Jim feels sad because his dog Muffins has been run over by a truck. The boy talks about his sadness with his family and friends. In the end they help Jim realize that sadness is natural and that there are things he can do to feel better. The brightly colored pictures relieve the feeling of sadness, making the reader believe that Jim will be all right. This is one in a series of books about Jim.

Genre: Realistic fiction
Subjects: Death; pets

COHEN, Miriam. *Tough Jim.*   Illus. by Lillian Hoban. Macmillan, 1974. ISBN: 0-027-22760-X
Everyone in the class has a costume for the party except Jim. At the last minute he decides what to wear, and his costume turns out to be the best of all. The costume even helps him get rid of a tough third grader, John Zoogfelder. In the end, Jim becomes the hero of the class. This is one in a series of books about Jim and his classmates.

Genre: Realistic fiction
Subject: Bullies

CREWS, Donald. *Harbor.*   Illus. by the author. Greenwillow, 1982. ISBN: 0-688-00862-3
Among the many kinds of ships in the harbor is a fireboat at work. The narrative is brief, giving the name of a ship on each page. Done in blocks of solid colors, the pictures focus attention on the shapes of the different ships.

Genre: Nonfiction
Subjects: Harbors; ships

DABCOVICH, Lydia. *Sleepy Bear.*   Illus. by the author. Dutton, 1982. ISBN: 0-525-44196-4

It is beginning to be cold and snowy outside. Bear decides it is time to hibernate and crawls into his house, intending to sleep through the cold weather. But Bear is in for a surprise, as something happens to make it get up.

Genre: Realistic fiction
Subject: Hibernation

DELTON, Judy. *I'm Telling You Now*.   Illus. by Lillian Hoban. Dutton, 1982. ISBN: 0-525-44037-2
Artie has a knack for getting into trouble. His mother keeps telling him not to do things he has already started. "Don't hang off the roof." "Don't cross the road." It seems she is always saying *don't*. When Artie protests, she just answers, "I'm telling you now." At last his mother agrees to let Artie do something he wants to do—he can dig a hole through the middle of the world.

Genre: Realistic fiction
Subject: Family life

DR. SEUSS. *The Cat in the Hat*.   Illus. by the author. Random House, 1957. ISBN: 0-394-80001-X
It's a rainy day, and Sally and her brother are wondering what to do. Then along comes a lively cat in a great big hat who wants to do tricks for them. The cat messes up the house, and when their mother comes home, Sally, her brother, and the cat will be in trouble. But just as mom arrives, the cat shows the children one more trick to save the day. Cartoonlike characters add comedy to this zany Seuss story, which is one in a series of books about the Cat in the Hat.

Genre: Fantasy
Subjects: Magic; cats; stories in rhyme; nonsense verses

DR. SEUSS. *The Cat in the Hat Comes Back*.   Illus. by the author. Random House, 1957. ISBN: 0-394-80001-X
The Cat in the Hat is back and up to his old mischief, eating cake in the bathtub and making a fine mess for Sally and her brother. It's almost time for their mother to come home and they must clean the house. As usual, the cat has something under its hat to help them—tiny cats in hats named A, B, C, D. . . . The big cat and the 26 miniature clones teach beginning readers the alphabet. The storyline also appeals to the more so-

phisticated reader. This is one in a series of books about the Cat in the Hat.

Genre: Fantasy

Subjects: Cats; stories in rhyme; alphabet

EHRLICH, Amy. *Leo, Zack, and Emmie.*   Illus. by Steve Kellogg. Dial, 1981. ISBN: 0-8037-4761-6

The new girl in the class, Emmie, is fun. She makes strange faces and can even wiggle her ears. In fact, she can do many things better than either Leo or Zack. Emmie is so much fun that both boys want to be her only friend. However, Emmie has other plans that lead everyone into trouble and then out again.

Genre: Realistic fiction

Subjects: Friendship; school stories

HOBAN, Lillian. *Arthur's Christmas Cookies.*   Illus. by the author. Harper & Row, 1984. ISBN: 0-06-022367-7

Arthur the chimpanzee decides to make Christmas cookies. But just as he is starting, his friends come in and, naturally, they want to help. The friends add and subtract ingredients that make the cookies beautiful but inedible. Now Arthur will have to find another use for them. The Christmas tree gives him an idea. This is one of a series of books about Arthur.

Genre: Realistic fiction

Subjects: Holidays (Christmas); chimpanzees

HOBAN, Lillian. *Arthur's Funny Money.*   Illus. by the author. Harper & Row, 1981. ISBN: 0-06-022343-X

Arthur the chimpanzee has become a Frisbee player. He needs to earn money for a team T-shirt but doesn't know what to do. His friends run errands for everyone he knows and wash all their cars. Arthur's sister has an idea that just might work, if all her friends don't get in the way. This is one in a series of books about Arthur.

Genre: Realistic fiction

Subjects: Business enterprises; chimpanzees

HOBAN, Lillian. *Arthur's Halloween Costume.*   Illus. by the author. Harper & Row, 1984. ISBN: 0-06-022387-1

It was starting to be a bad day for Arthur the chimpanzee, even though it was Halloween. His sister Violet had eaten almost all the chicken soup for lunch. He had lost his homework, and now he had spilled ketchup on his ghost costume. Arthur didn't have anything else to wear for the school Halloween party. In the end a cat comes to the rescue, and Arthur goes to the party in an original costume. Illustrated by pencil drawings filled with soft shades of yellows, oranges, purples, and pinks, this story is one in a series of books about Arthur.

Genre: Realistic fiction
Subjects: Chimpanzees; holidays (Halloween)

HOFF, Syd. *Barkley.* Illus. by the author. Harper & Row, 1975. ISBN: 0-06-022448-7
Barkley has always been a circus dog, but he's getting old. The owners of the circus don't want an old dog around anymore. This saddens Barkley and he tries to find some way to be useful. Just when he is about to give up, there is a problem at the circus. Readers can guess who rushes to the rescue and becomes a valuable member of the circus once more. Simple green and brown illustrations capture the sadness of being rejected.

Genre: Realistic fiction
Subjects: Dogs; circuses

HUTCHINS, Pat. *The Wind Blew.* Illus. by the author. Macmillan, 1974. ISBN: 0-02-745910-1
On a day when everyone in the village seems to be out of doors, a big wind strikes. It takes a hat from one person, a scarf from another, mail from the mail carrier's bag, and wigs, umbrellas, and balloons from other people. The wind even carries off flags from the flagpoles and newspapers from the village yards. Soon everyone in the village is chasing something taken by the fierce wind. But then, as quickly as it came, the wind moves out to sea, leaving the village and its people in a terrible mess.

Genre: Realistic fiction
Subjects: Wind; neighbors

ISADORA, Rachel. *Max.* Illus. by the author. Macmillan, 1976. ISBN: 0-02-747450-X

Like many boys, Max would rather play baseball than almost anything in the world. In fact, Max is about to play a game when his sister invites him to her dance class. He goes just to see what is happening there, but is soon swept into the action. Max has become a dance student by accident. Through his experience in dance class he now knows how to warm up for the game each week so he can give his best baseball performance.

Genre: Realistic fiction
Subjects: Ballet; baseball

JOHNSTON, Tony. *Farmer Mack Measures His Pig.*   Illus. by the author. Harper & Row, 1986. ISBN: 0-06-023017-7
Farmer Mack has a very big pig, and so does his neighbor. Deciding which pig is bigger is the subject of much argument. Farmer Mack decides that measuring his pig is the only way to find out how big it really is. But how can he measure an animal that is so big and round as his pig? His efforts lead to one problem after another as the story unfolds.

Genre: Realistic fiction
Subjects: Farmers; pigs

JONAS, Ann. *Two Bear Cubs.*   Illus. by the author. Greenwillow, 1982. ISBN: 0-688-01407-0
Two bear cubs, out with their mother hunting for food, become separated from her. While on their own, the cubs have many problems, including trying to get honey from a tree and fish from a stream. But the worst of their troubles is with a skunk. The curious cubs follow the skunk a bit too closely and learn a bitter lesson before being rescued by their mother.

Genre: Realistic fiction
Subject: Bears

KANTROWITZ, Mildred. *Willy Bear.*   Illus. by Nancy Winslow Parker. Macmillan, 1980. ISBN: 0-02-749790-9
It is the night before the first day of school, and a boy is filled with fears about what the next day will bring. He has just one comfort for the long night, his old friend Willy Bear, a teddy bear. The boy shares his troubles with the bear and in doing so finds a way to allay his fears. Illustrated by line drawings in soft pastels, the story shows how the boy manages to adjust to his first day of school.

Genre: Realistic fiction
Subjects: Teddy bears; school stories; fear
Award: Christopher Awards Children's Book Category, 1976 picture book

KEATS, Ezra Jack. *A Letter to Amy.* Illus. by the author. Harper & Row, 1968. ISBN: 0-06-443063-4
Peter is having a birthday party and wants to invite his friend Amy, who would be the only girl. Because Peter feels he can't talk to Amy about the party, he decides to write her a special invitation. It's stormy outside when Peter sets out to mail the letter. A gust of wind carries the letter off, and as Peter chases it, he gets into trouble. He is especially embarrassed when he meets Amy during the chase. This is one in a series of stories about Peter and his friends.

Genre: Realistic fiction
Subjects: Friendship; letter writing

KEATS, Ezra Jack. *Regards to the Man in the Moon.* Illus. by the author. Four Winds, 1981. ISBN: 0-590-07820-8
Louie's friends always tease him because he collects junk. But Louie feels that with the junk and some imagination, he and his friends can do almost anything, even explore space. However, when they use the junk to make a spaceship and begin their exploration, their imaginations take them into unusual situations that include a rescue in space.

Genre: Realistic fiction
Subjects: Boys; imagination; space

KRAUS, Robert. *Whose Mouse Are You?* Illus. by Jose Aruego. Macmillan, 1970. ISBN: 0-02-751190-1
Mouse belongs to no one. His mother is inside a cat, his father is trapped, and his sister has moved far away. Mouse wishes he had a brother and that his family was back, too. In the story of the family's rescue, Mouse finds himself richer than before. Not only does the family come back but there is also someone new.

Genre: Realistic fiction
Subjects: Mice; family life; stories in rhyme

LeSIEG, Theo. *The Tooth Book.* Illus. by Roy McKie. Random House, 1981. ISBN: 0-394-94825-4

Written in rhyme and illustrated with cartoon drawings, this book teaches young readers about the different kinds of teeth. It uses rhythmic language to explain who has teeth and what they're used for, and encourages readers to take care of their teeth.

Genre: Nonfiction
Subjects: Teeth; stories in rhyme

LEWIS, Thomas P. *Mr. Sniff and the Motel Mystery.*   Illus. by Beth Weiner Woldin. Harper & Row, 1984. ISBN: 0-06-023824-0
Someone has put a jellyfish in the motel swimming pool. It is a mystery that demands the skills of the great dog detective, Mr. Sniff. The dog begins to investigate, looking everywhere for the solution to the mystery, but without success. In the end the mystery is solved with the aid of a piece of bubble gum. This is one in a series of mystery stories about the determined Mr. Sniff.

Genre: Mystery
Subject: Dogs

LEXAU, Joan. *The Rooftop Mystery.*   Illus. by Syd Hoff. Harper & Row, 1968. ISBN: 0-06-023865-8
Sam's little sister has lost her doll. He agrees to find it, but he gets more help than he needs from Albert and Amy Lou. After a great deal of trouble and many false clues, the doll is finally dis-covered — on the rooftop. Cartoonlike drawings in rust and blue add humor to this lighthearted story. This is one in a series of books about Sam.

Genre: Mystery
Subjects: Family life; dolls

LOBEL, Arnold. *Days with Frog and Toad.*   Illus. by the author. Harper & Row, 1979. ISBN: 0-06-023964-6
In five short stories about two old friends, Frog and Toad, the readers are told about their experiences with a kite, a cold, and being alone. There is a story about what tomorrow will bring and one about a very special birthday hat. Whatever the adven-ture, Frog and Toad always seem to work things out together. This is one in a series of books about these two endearing com-panions.

Genre: Humor
Subjects: Frogs; toads; friendship
Award: George G. Stone Center for Children's Books Recognition of Merit, 1978

LOBEL, Arnold. *Ming Lo Moves the Mountain.* Illus. by the author. Greenwillow, 1982. ISBN: 0-688-00610-8
Ming Lo and his wife live in a beautiful house by a high mountain. Everything is fine until they discover that the mountain blocks the sun so that the house is always dark. Ming Lo decides that something must be done, so he visits the wise man. The story ends happily when Ming Lo finds a way to move the mountain. Soft watercolors illustrate the story.

Genre: Humor
Subjects: Mountains; dwellings; folklore

LOBEL, Arnold. *Owl at Home.* Illus. by the author. Harper & Row, 1975. ISBN: 0-06-023948-4
Five separate adventures of a silly owl begin with fears that lead to imagined thumpings under Owl's bed. A pushy visitor comes to Owl's home to start trouble in the second story. The next two adventures lead to the final chapter in which Owl has even more trouble as he prepares for winter. Line sketches washed with muted browns and grays illustrate the stories.

Genre: Humor
Subject: Owls
Award: Garden State Children's Book Award, 1978

LOBEL, Arnold. *Small Pig.* Illus. by the author. Harper & Row, 1969. ISBN: 0-06-023932-8
Small Pig is the pet of the entire farm family, and it is very happy until the farmer's wife decides to clean everything. A pigsty without mud is no fun at all, so the unhappy pig runs away. Not prepared for the traffic and city problems, he finds a "mud" hole just the right size in the middle of a sidewalk. It is strange, oozy "mud" that Small Pig settles in, and while the pig sleeps, the cement hardens. Everything turns out happily when the family comes in search of their pet and rescues Small Pig from a serious predicament. Very simple illustrations help young readers

through the story and entertain them with the delightfully humorous expressions on Small Pig's face.

Genre: Humor
Subjects: Pigs; pets

LOBEL, Arnold. *Uncle Elephant.*   Illus. by the author. Harper & Row, 1981. ISBN: 0-06-023979-4
The story opens on a sad day for Little Elephant. His parents have gone off in a ship, and the ship with his parents is missing. Little Elephant is all alone and frightened. Then along comes wrinkled old Uncle Elephant to care for the abandoned baby. Uncle Elephant knows what to do, even after receiving the telegram about Little Elephant's family.

Genre: Adventure
Subjects: Fear; families; uncles; elephants

LOPSHIRE, Robert. *Put Me in the Zoo.*   Illus. by the author. Random House, 1960. ISBN: 0-394-80017-6
A big yellow animal wants to be in the zoo, but the zookeepers won't let it in. The animal meets a boy and girl and proceeds to tell them in rhyme why the zookeepers should change their minds. The animal has large, bright dots on its skin and shows the children how it can move the dots—put them on something else, change their colors, juggle them. After all these demonstrations, the children decide there's a better place for this animal than the zoo. The animal takes their advice and is happy there.

Genre: Fantasy
Subjects: Stories in rhyme; animals

LUND, Doris. *You Ought to See Herbert's House.*   Illus. by Steven Kellogg. Franklin Watts, 1973. ISBN: 0-531-02595-0 (o.p.)
Herbert says he lives in a house with three flags on top and water surrounding it. At least that is what he tells his new friend, Roger. His story is not exactly true, as Roger sees for himself when he spends the night at Herbert's house. However, Roger discovers that the house does have some strange pets and an unusual place to sleep.

Genre: Realistic fiction
Subjects: Friendship; imagination

McPHAIL, David. *Emma's Pet.* Illus. by the author. Dutton, 1985. ISBN: 0-525-44210-3
Emma already has a pet but searches everywhere for another one. She wants the new pet to be big and cuddly but can't seem to find one that suits her. Emma looks everywhere and finally meets with success right in her own house, where she finds a highly unusual pet that exactly fits her dreams. Clear, detailed pictures colored mostly in pastels illustrate the story and its surprise ending.

Genre: Realistic fiction
Subject: Family life

McPHAIL, David. *Great Cat.* Illus. by the author. Dutton, 1982. ISBN: 0-525-45102-1
Unlike other cats, this one seems to keep growing. It's the biggest cat anyone has ever seen, and it's not cuddly or easily petted. The other cats are afraid to play cat games with it. Thus Great Cat is lonely and sees no purpose in life. Then a fire occurs, and Great Cat and the other animals find that its large size has some advantages.

Genre: Fantasy
Subjects: Cats; loneliness

MARSHALL, Edward. *Fox and His Friends.* Illus. by James Marshall. Dial, 1982. ISBN: 0-8037-0001-6
In three separate episodes, Fox wants to play with his friends but duty always interferes. His work as a crossing guard presents the first problem, then his mother insists that he take care of Louise, his younger sister. Louise knows Fox doesn't like high places, so why is she at the top of that telephone pole, and how did she get up to that high diving board? This is one in a series of amusing books about the escapades of Fox and his friends.

Genre: Humor
Subjects: Foxes; brothers and sisters; friendship

MARSHALL, Edward. *Fox on Wheels.* Illus. by James Marshall. Dial, 1982. ISBN: 0-8037-2668-6
As always, Fox has to take care of his little sister Louise, but he's not doing it very well. In the first of three short stories, Louise has a chance to trick Fox. Then his friend Millie tricks Fox into

climbing a tree. Still the problems with his sister and Millie seem small compared to his trouble when his friends have a shopping-cart race in the supermarket. There is a quiet humor to each of the episodes in this action-filled book. This is one in a series of books about the escapades of Fox and his friends.

Genre: Humor
Subjects: Foxes; brothers and sisters

MARSHALL, Edward. *Three by the Sea.* Illus. by James Marshall. Dial, 1981. ISBN: 0-8037-8687-6
Lolly, Sam, and Spider sit on the beach and tell stories, each trying to tell a more exciting one than the last. Lolly's story is about a rat and cat, but her friends say it's dull. Sam tells another story, but Spider does not like the ending. Finally, it's time to listen to Spider, whose story about the cat and the rat includes a monster and an ending that scares Lolly and Sam.

Genre: Humor
Subject: Storytelling

MARSHALL, James. *George and Martha, Back in Town.* Illus. by the author. Houghton Mifflin, 1984. ISBN: 0-395-35386-6
Five brief stories relate the adventures of two hippos, George and Martha, who seem to be always in trouble. In one story, they have an exciting experience with Mexican jumping beans. Then George decides to be a high diver, but needs Martha's help. Later they play tricks on each other like nailing shoes to the floor. The last two stories are about a job as a lifeguard and an experience with reading that leads to a lesson in being considerate. This is one in a series of comical books about these two great friends.

Genre: Humor
Subjects: Hippopotamuses; friendship

MARSHALL, James. *George and Martha One Fine Day.* Illus. by the author. Houghton Mifflin, 1978. ISBN: 0-395-27154-1
In the first of five stories, Martha the Hippo walks a tightrope. Her friend George is explaining why he never would, but Martha shouldn't listen or she might fall. The other episodes are about keeping a diary, telling a disquieting story, going to an amusement park, and the big scare. The book begins with George upsetting Martha, but Martha gets the best of George in the end.

This is one in a series of comical books about these two great friends.

Genre: Humor
Subjects: Hippopotamuses; friendship

MARSHALL, James. *The Guest.*   Illus. by the author. Houghton Mifflin, 1975. ISBN: 0-395-20277-9
Mona, a strange, big, gray animal, was lonely until Maurice the snail came to live with her. When Maurice disappears, Mona is lonely again and looks even sadder than before. However, when Maurice returns, it is easy to see why he left. Now Maurice is leading his large family of snails into Mona's house. The contrast between big, sad, gray Mona and the bright, pink snail with all its little snails pleases even the youngest of readers.

Genre: Fantasy
Subjects: Animals; friendship; snails

MODELL, Frank. *One Zillion Valentines.*   Illus. by the author. Greenwillow, 1981. ISBN: 0-688-00565-9
It will soon be Valentine's Day, and Marvin and Milton do not have money to buy cards for their friends. The two boys decide to make the valentines. The problem is that Marvin and Milton can't seem to stop. After making about a zillion valentines, the boys decide to go into business, and they are so successful they end up without any valentines to give each other. But now that they have money, there is a solution to this problem, too.

Genre: Realistic fiction
Subjects: Holidays (Valentine's Day); friendship

OXENBURY, Helen. *The Dancing Class.*   Illus. by the author. Dial, 1983. ISBN: 0-8037-1651-6
The girl in this story is wild about dancing. She finally gets to go to dance class and is so excited that she doesn't tie her shoes well. In the middle of a dance, a shoe comes untied and the girl trips over the lace. As if this isn't embarrassing enough, her fall starts a chain reaction that upsets the whole dance class. Small sketches capture the girl's excitement as well as her misery.

Genre: Realistic fiction
Subject: Ballet

PARISH, Peggy. *Dinosaur Time.*   Illus. by Arnold Lobel. Harper & Row, 1974. ISBN: 0-06-024653-7
Young readers seem to have a natural interest in dinosaurs that is well satisfied by this book. The author describes 11 dinosaurs, pronouncing their names, comparing their sizes, and giving information about the foods they ate. The outstanding illustrations show how the dinosaurs might have looked.

Genre: Nonfiction
Subject: Dinosaurs

PARKER, Nancy Winslow. *Poofy Loves Company.*   Illus. by the author. Dodd, Mead, 1980. ISBN: 0-396-00783-8
Sally and her mother visit a friend with a big dog, Poofy. The dog becomes very attached to Sally but has an odd way of showing its affection. Stealing her balloon and snatching her cookie are only two of the tricks Poofy plays.

Genre: Realistic fiction
Subject: Dogs

PLATT, Kin. *Big Max in the Mystery of the Missing Moose.* Illus. by Robert Lopshire. Harper & Row, 1977. ISBN: 0-06-024756-8
Mr. Zonker, the zookeeper, has a problem—Marvin the moose has run away! Big Max, the detective, looks everywhere for Marvin. Some of the zoo animals have seen a moose pass by, but no one seems to know where to find him. Still, the detective follows the clues and manages to track down Marvin just in time. This is the second book in a series about Big Max.

Genre: Mystery
Subjects: Animals; moose

POMERANTZ, Charlotte. *The Piggy in the Puddle.*   Illus. by James Marshall. Macmillan, 1977. ISBN: 0-02-774900-2
Someone is misbehaving in this family of pigs. The parents cannot get their little pig to come out of the mud. In fact, Little Pig is having so much fun that perhaps his parents should join in. If Little Pig's big brother gets into the act, then everyone in the family will be happily wallowing in the mud puddle.

Genre: Humor
Subjects: Pigs; stories in rhyme

RASKIN, Ellen. *And It Rained.* Illus. by the author. Atheneum, 1969. ISBN: 0-689-20587-2 (o.p.)
Every afternoon at four o'clock the animals try to have tea, but just when they begin their tea, it starts to rain continuously. All the animals are disappointed until one of them, the potto, comes up with a way to make the four o'clock tea a real success. The finely detailed pictures place green foregrounds against alternating yellow and blue backgrounds.

Genre: Fantasy
Subjects: Animals; rain

REY, H. A. *Curious George.* Illus. by the author. Houghton Mifflin, 1941. ISBN: 0-395-15023-X
George the monkey travels from Africa to America to jail. The Man in the Yellow Hat has a hard time keeping track of the trouble-making monkey. Whatever the consequences, George seems determined to find out just how things work. His curiosity carries him from one adventure to the next, until finally he lands in what seems to be the perfect place. This is one in a series of stories about the inquisitive monkey.

Genre: Adventure
Subject: Monkeys

REY, Margaret and H. A. Rey. *Curious George Flies a Kite.* Illus. by H. A. Rey. Houghton Mifflin, 1958. ISBN: 0-395-25937-1
Curious George is a monkey who just has to try everything, from holding a baby rabbit to catching fish to flying a kite. But the rabbit runs away, George tries to catch the fish with a piece of cake, and then the Man in the Yellow Hat has to rescue the kite-flying monkey in a helicopter. This is one in a series of books about the adventures of Curious George.

Genre: Adventure
Subject: Monkeys

RICCIUTI, Edward R. *Donald and the Fish That Walked.* Illus. by Syd Hoff. Harper & Row, 1974. ISBN: 0-06-024998-6
Donald really did see a pink fish walking on the lawn, or so he said. No one believed him until some adults found some walk-

ing fish, too. Then a cold spell seemed to have killed the strange fish, but it had done something very different after all.

Genre: Realistic fiction
Subject: Fish

RICE, Eve. *Papa's Lemonade and Other Stories.*   Illus. by the author. Greenwillow, 1976. ISBN: 0-688-80041-6 (o.p.)
Freddie, Molly, Sam, Nora, Jasper, Mama, and Papa are the members of this dog family. They're always trying something new in the five episodes that make up this book. No one knows what to do with a piggy bank, and they try to make lemonade from oranges. It's just one mix-up after another as the story develops from its start at the lemonade stand.

Genre: Humor
Subjects: Dogs; family life

RYLANT, Cynthia. *Henry and Mudge: The First Book of Their Adventures.*   Illus. by Sucie Stevenson. Bradbury, 1987. ISBN: 0-02-778001-5
Living on a street without other children, Henry feels lonely until he finds companionship in a dog named Mudge. Henry loves everything about Mudge, and Mudge loves everything about Henry—from his socks to his fish tank to his bed. Both characters are miserable when Mudge becomes lost. The illustrations shift from Henry to Mudge, allowing the reader to share their feelings. This is the first in a series of books about Henry and Mudge.

Genre: Realistic fiction
Subjects: Dogs; friendship; pets

SCHATELL, Brian. *Sam's No Dummy, Farmer Goff.*   Illus. by the author. Lippincott, 1984. ISBN: 0-397-32061-2
Sam the turkey is a very tiresome animal to have around—or so thinks Farmer Goff, who wakes up when Sam "moos" and "meows" and "oinks" in the middle of the night. The farmer is so angry he threatens to eat the turkey for Thanksgiving dinner. But then he decides to become famous by putting the turkey on television. Sam's refusal to perform leads to a wild uproar and the chance that Farmer Goff will eat Sam for Thanksgiving dinner after all. In the end Sam manages to save the day and his own

skin. Drawings in browns and rusts help establish the feeling of autumn. This is one in a series of books about Farmer Goff and his turkey, Sam.

Genre: Humor
Subject: Turkeys

SHARMAT, Marjorie Weinman. *Burton and Dudley.* Illus. by Barbara Cooney. Avon, 1977. ISBN: 0-380-01732-6
Burton just wants to sit by the window, but his friend Dudley would rather take a walk—for 20 miles. Burton is not happy about the idea, but he goes along. The two oppossums see a great many things that Burton had never seen just sitting by the window. In the end, Dudley is worn out and would rather stay home, and Burton is so excited about his adventure that he wants to go out again.

Genre: Adventure
Subjects: Opossums; friendship

SHARMAT, Marjorie Weinman. *Nate the Great and the Sticky Case.* Illus. by Marc Simont. Coward, 1978. ISBN: 0-698-30697-X
Nate may be the greatest detective of all, but this case certainly has him stumped. He thinks it will be easy to find a lost dinosaur, imagining one that's so big it would be hard to miss. The great detective is in for quite a surprise when he sees the size of this dinosaur. Nate and his friends, Claude, Annie, Rosamond, and Sludge, are all caught up in this mystery. This is one in a series of books about the young detective.

Genre: Mystery
Subject: Dinosaurs

SPIER, Peter. *Bored, Nothing to Do.* Illus. by the author. Doubleday, 1978. ISBN: 0-385-13177-1
It is just one of those days when there is nothing to do, so the two brothers in this story use their imaginations to do something. They confiscate a few of the family's possessions—the wheels from the baby buggy, their mother's sheets, the engine from the car—to make an airplane that takes them on a wild, imaginary trip.

Genre: Fantasy
Subjects: Play; creation (literary, artistic, etc.); airplanes

STEVENSON, James. *Fast Friends*. Illus. by the author. Greenwillow, 1979. ISBN: 0-688-80197-8

The two stories in this book are about friends. In the first story, Murray the turtle and Fred the snail make friends with the help of a skateboard that they don't know how to stop. In the second story, Thomas the mouse and Clem the turtle learn about the meaning of being friends.

Genre: Realistic fiction
Subjects: Animals; friendship

STEVENSON, James. *Howard*. Illus. by the author. Greenwillow, 1980. ISBN: 0-688-84255-0

All the other ducks have flown away, leaving Howard behind, so he tries to catch up but gets lost. Stranded in New York in the winter, the duck meets three mice and a frog, but he is still lonely. He finds it hard to make friends when there are no other ducks around. Yet, as the story unfolds, Howard finds a very special friend. This is a warm and humorous tale with an unexpected ending. New York City is pictured in detailed line and watercolor drawings.

Genre: Humor
Subjects: Ducks; New York City; friendship
Award: *New York Times* Choice of Best Illustrated Children's Book, 1980

STEVENSON, James. *Monty*. Illus. by the author. Greenwillow, 1979. ISBN: 0-688-84209-7

Every day Monty the alligator gives his friends a ride across the river to school. The rabbit, the duck, and the frog order the alligator to go faster, to swim smoother, and to turn. One day Monty grows tired of being taken for granted and goes on vacation. Now there is no way for his three friends to get to school. They make some laughable tries at crossing the river and then come to appreciate the alligator. Meanwhile, Monty is doing some thinking of his own that brings his vacation and their dilemma to an end. This is one in a series of books about the adventures of Monty.

Genre: Humor
Subjects: Alligators; appreciation; friendship

STEVENSON, James. *That Dreadful Day.* Illus. by the author. Greenwillow, 1985. ISBN: 0-688-04036-5
Based on Grandpa's wild memories, this story begins when Mary Ann and Louis worry about their first day at school. Grandpa protests that their adventure couldn't possibly be as bad as the horrible day he remembers. This is one in a series of books about what Grandpa remembers when Mary Ann and Louie are faced with problems.

Genre: Fantasy
Subjects: School stories; grandfathers

STEVENSON, James. *That Terrible Halloween Night.* Illus. by the author. Greenwillow, 1980. ISBN: 0-688-80281-8
This promises to be a scary night for Louie, Mary Ann, and Leonard. Grandpa is sure it can't be any scarier than that terrible Halloween he experienced, when he was swept away by a storm and so badly frightened that his hair turned white over night. This is one in a series about what Grandpa remembers.

Genre: Fantasy
Subjects: Fantasy; families

THALER, Mike. *Owly.* Illus. by David Wiesner. Harper & Row, 1982. ISBN: 0-06-026151-X
The little owl is full of questions that his mother doesn't answer. He wants to know how many stars are in the sky, so his mother tells him to count them. Her advice is the same when he wonders how many waves are in the ocean. So Little Owl counts and counts and counts. By the end of the story he still doesn't know how many stars are in the sky or how many waves are in the ocean. But he has found a way to tell his mother how much he loves her.

Genre: Realistic fiction
Subjects: Parents and children; owls

THAYER, Jane. *Popcorn Dragon.* Illus. by Jay Hyde Barnum. Morrow, 1953. ISBN: 0-688-21630-7 (o.p.)
This is a really nice dragon who wants to be a friend to everyone. But no one believes that because this dragon breathes hot air and fire. Wandering around sadly looking for a playmate, the dragon finally rests beside an ear of corn. The little dragon's world

changes when his neighbors smell the popcorn that comes from his breathing hot air on that ear of corn.

Genre: Fantasy
Subjects: Dragons; loneliness

VAN LEEUWEN, Jean. *Amanda Pig and Her Big Brother Oliver.*   Illus. by Ann Schweninger. Dial, 1982. ISBN: 0-8037-0016-4
Amanda Pig is the small sister who wants to do everything her big brother Oliver can do. Although Amanda tries her best, there is nothing but trouble in the five stories that fill this book. The same characters are featured in other books about the Pig family.

Genre: Realistic fiction
Subjects: Brothers and sisters; pigs

VAN WOERKOM, Dorothy. *Harry and Shelburt.*   Illus. by Erick Ingraham. Macmillan, 1977. ISBN: 0-02-791290-6 (o.p.)
Harry Hare and Shelburt Tortoise are good friends until Shelburt tells a story about a race a turtle won long ago. Harry has a hard time believing turtles can win, so he and Shelburt agree to run the race again. The outcome is predictable to anyone who knows about tortoises and hares.

Genre: Humor
Subjects: Rabbits; turtles; friendship

VINCENT, Gabrielle. *Bravo, Ernest and Celestine!*   Illus. by the author. Greenwillow, 1982. ISBN: 0-688-00857-7
Ernest the bear and Celestine the mouse need to fix a leaky roof. Celestine is sure that Ernest can earn the money they need by playing his violin. Ernest plays, but no one pays to hear him, so Celestine has another idea. This is one in a series of books starring Ernest and Celestine, the unlikely pair of bear and mouse friends.

Genre: Fantasy
Subjects: Bears; mice; friendship

VINCENT, Gabrielle. *Ernest and Celestine.*   Illus. by the author. Greenwillow, 1982. ISBN: 0-688-00855-0
Celestine thinks every mouse should have a bear friend like Ernest. When she loses her doll, Ernest helps her find it. The

doll is completely ruined but Ernest helps to fix the problem. The two friends move from one solution to another as they bungle their way through the story to its warm and happy ending. This is one in a series of books starring Ernest and Celestine.

Genre: Fantasy

Subjects: Bears; mice; friendship

VINCENT, Gabrielle. *Merry Christmas, Ernest and Celestine.* Illus. by the author. Greenwillow, 1984. ISBN: 0-688-02605-2
It's almost Christmas and Ernest the bear is in trouble. He has no money, but Celestine the mouse insists that he give a Christmas party. He promised he would, and friends should keep their promises. In the end, Celestine gets her party and a surprise visit from a familiar-looking Santa Claus. This is one in a series of books about Ernest and Celestine.

Genre: Fantasy

Subjects: Holidays (Christmas); bears; mice; friendship

VINCENT, Gabrielle. *Smile, Ernest and Celestine.* Illus. by the author. Greenwillow, 1982. ISBN: 0-688-01247-7
Celestine the mouse is angry. She thought Ernest the bear was a special friend. So why does he have so many pictures of other friends? There are no pictures of Celestine in his drawer. Of course, this omission is easily remedied — but not without other misadventures as the two friends quarrel and then make up. This is part of a series of books about the adventures of Ernest and Celestine.

Genre: Fantasy

Subjects: Bears; mice; friendship

WABER, Bernard. *Ira Sleeps Over.* Illus. by the author. Houghton Mifflin, 1972. ISBN: 0-395-13893-0
Ira is going to his friend Reggie's house to sleep over. He wants to take the teddy bear he always sleeps with but is afraid his sister and Reggie will laugh. While at Reggie's house, Ira and Reggie have great fun playing games until it's time to turn out the lights and face the moment of truth. All ends happily, though, as Ira learns something about Reggie that stills his own fears.

Genre: Realistic fiction

Subjects: Friendship; toys; bedtime

WELLS, Rosemary. *A Lion for Lewis.*   Illus. by the author. Dial, 1982. ISBN: 0-8037-4683-0
Sophie and George are putting on a play. They don't think their little brother Lewis is capable of doing much in their play, so he only gets small parts. Then Lewis discovers something in the attic that changes their minds. Illustrated in soft watercolors, the story exposes the trials and tribulations of being the youngest as Lewis takes matters into his own hands.

Genre: Realistic fiction
Subjects: Brothers and sisters; play

WELLS, Rosemary. *Max's First Word.*   Illus. by the author. Dial, 1979. ISBN: 0-8037-6066-3
Ruby wants baby rabbit Max to talk, but all Max says is "bang." She is about to give up when Max surprises her and brings the story to a funny ending by finally saying another word. This is one in a series of books about the things Max learns.

Genre: Humor
Subjects: Vocabulary; brothers and sisters; rabbits

WISEMAN, Bernard. *Hooray for Patsy's Oink!*   Illus. by the author. Garrard, 1980. ISBN: 8116-6079-6
Patsy Pig thinks she would like to be someone else, so she waddles around the farm trying to sound like each animal. Needless to say, all the animals are happy with the sound Patsy finally settles on making.

Genre: Realistic fiction
Subjects: Animals; self-esteem

WISEMAN, Bernard. *Morris Goes to School.*   Illus. by the author. Harper & Row, 1970. ISBN 0-06-026548-5
Morris the moose has six pennies to buy gumdrops, and they cost a penny a piece. He can't figure out how many his money will buy, so Morris goes to school. As far as the moose is concerned, it hardly matters that he's too noisy and doesn't quite fit in the chairs. The important thing is that he finally learns all the *numbers* in the *alphabet*. This is one in a series of books about the silly moose.

Genre: Humor
Subjects: Moose; school

WISEMAN, Bernard. *Morris Tells Boris Mother Moose Stories and Rhymes.* Illus. by the author. Dodd, Mead, 1979. ISBN: 0-396-07693-9

In the laughable style that characterizes their friendship, Morris the moose agrees to tell Boris the bear a story to help him go to sleep. Boris wants a Mother Goose story, but Morris insists on including himself or Boris in each story. So the stories and rhymes become the Four Bears, the Moose Ran Up the Clock, and on and on—until Boris decides to go to sleep. This is one in a series of books about the exploits of Morris.

Genre: Humor
Subject: Mother Goose stories

WOLCOTT, Patty. *Pickle, Pickle, Pickle Juice.* Illus. by Blair Drawson. Harper & Row, 1975. ISBN: 0-201-14252-X

Peter wants to pick a pickle, but that pickle leads to one after another. Now he has picked a few too many, and juice is pouring out. He has created a pickle juice stream and a pickle juice lake. The illustrations in the book flow with green as the stream of pickle juice covers the countryside.

Genre: Fantasy
Subjects: Boys; pickles

YOLEN, Jane. *Mice on Ice.* Illus. by Lawrence Di Fiori. Dutton, 1980. ISBN: 0-525-34872-7

The Mice Capades are a big hit. But trouble brews because Gomer the rat is jealous. He plans to kidnap the star and hold her for ransom. The question is, will Gomer succeed? The story has all the ingredients readers enjoy—a chase, a heroine, humor. There's even an element of ice-making magic.

Genre: Adventure
Subjects: Ice skating; kidnapping; mice

4

Books for the First Half of Grade Two
Readability: 2.0–2.4

Children in the second grade have greatly expanded vocabularies. As they study in school and have different experiences outside of school, their interests include a broader range of subjects. This list includes a range from very simple to complex topics.

EASY

Alexander, Martha. *We're in Big Trouble, Blackboard Bear*
Asch, Frank. *Happy Birthday, Moon*
———. *Moon Bear*
———. *Mooncake*
Babbitt, Natalie. *The Something*
Benchley, Nathaniel. *The Strange Disappearance of Arthur Cluck*
Brandenberg, Franz. *Leo and Emily's Big Ideas*
Brown, Margaret Wise. *Runaway Bunny*
Burningham, John. *Come Away from the Water, Shirley*
———. *The Shopping Basket*
dePaola, Tomie. *Things to Make and Do for Valentine's Day*
De Regniers, Beatrice Schenk. *Red Riding Hood*
Galdone, Paul. *The Three Little Pigs*
Ginsburg, Mirra. *Good Morning, Chick*
Hamilton, Morse and Emily Hamilton. *My Name Is Emily*
Hoff, Syd. *Danny and the Dinosaur*
Kellogg, Steven. *The Mystery of the Missing Red Mitten*
———. *The Mystery of the Stolen Blue Paint*

EASY (cont.)

McPhail, David. *The Train*

Modell, Frank. *Seen Any Cats?*

Nakatani, Chiyoko. *The Zoo in My Garden*

Nødset, Joan L. *Come Here, Cat*

Preston, Edna Mitchell. *Squawk to the Moon, Little Goose*

Rey, H. A. and Margaret Rey. *Curious George Goes to the Hospital*

Rockwell, Anne. *Poor Goose*

Sharmat, Marjorie Weinman. *Nate the Great and the Missing Key*

———. *Nate the Great and the Snowy Trail*

Slobodkina, Esphyr. *Caps for Sale*

Wells, Rosemary. *Max's New Suit*

Williams, Barbara. *Albert's Toothache*

AVERAGE

Ahlberg, Janet and Allan Ahlberg. *Funnybones*

Aliki. *Keep Your Mouth Closed, Dear*

Andersen, Hans Christian. *The Princess and the Pea*

Asbjornsen, P. C. and J. E. Moe. *The Three Billy Goats Gruff*

Bang, Molly Garrett. *Wiley and the Hairy Man*

Bemelmans, Ludwig. *Madeleine*

Benchley, Nathaniel. *George the Drummer Boy*

Bond, Felicia. *Poinsettia and the Firefighters*

Bonsall, Crosby Newell. *Tell Me Some More*

Burningham, John. *Mr. Gumpy's Motor Car*

———. *Mr. Gumpy's Outing*

Calhoun, Mary. *Hot Air Henry*

Chapman, Carol. *The Tale of Meshka the Kvetch*

Coerr, Eleanor. *The Big Balloon Race*

Dabcovich, Lydia. *Follow the River*

Delton, Judy. *Two Good Friends*

Duvoisin, Roger. *Petunia*

Gackenbach, Dick. *Harry and the Terrible Whatzit*

Gage, Wilson. *Squash Pie*

Galdone, Paul. *The Gingerbread Boy*

Hoban, Russell. *Dinner at Alberta's*

———. *Nothing to Do*

Hutchins, Pat. *You'll Soon Grow into Them, Titch*

Jonas, Ann. *The Quilt*

Keats, Ezra Jack. *Dreams*
———. *The Snowy Day*
Keller, Holly. *Geraldine's Blanket*
Krasilovsky, Phyllis. *The Man Who Entered a Contest*
Kroll, Steven. *One Tough Turkey*
Leaf, Munro. *The Story of Ferdinand*
Lobel, Arnold. *A Treeful of Pigs*
Locker, Thomas. *The Mare on the Hill*
Mahy, Margaret. *The Boy Who Was Followed Home*
Marshall, Edward. *Troll Country*
Morris, Robert A. *Seahorse*
Noble, Trinka Hakes. *The Day Jimmy's Boa Ate the Wash*
———. *Jimmy's Boa Bounces Back*
Parish, Peggy. *Amelia Bedelia Helps Out*
Quin-Harkin, Janet. *Helpful Hattie*
Rice, Eve. *Benny Bakes a Cake*
Sendak, Maurice. *In the Night Kitchen*
Sharmat, Marjorie Weinman. *Griselda's New Year*
Shulevitz, Uri. *Dawn*
Van Woerkom, Dorothy. *Donkey Ysabel*
Waber, Bernard. *An Anteater Named Arthur*
Wells, Rosemary. *Benjamin & Tulip*
Wiseman, Bernard. *Morris and Boris*
Zion, Gene. *Harry the Dirty Dog*
Zolotow, Charlotte. *Mr. Rabbit and the Lovely Present*

CHALLENGING

Allard, Harry. *Miss Nelson Is Back*
———. *Miss Nelson Is Missing*
Baker, Betty. *The Pig War*
Beim, Lorraine and Jerrold Beim. *The Little Igloo*
Blaine, Marge. *The Terrible Thing That Happened at Our House*
Blume, Judy. *The Pain and the Great One*
Brandenberg, Franz. *Nice New Neighbors*
Calhoun, Mary. *Cross-Country Cat*
dePaola, Tomie. *Watch Out for the Chicken Feet in Your Soup*
Hoban, Russell. *A Bargain for Frances*
Jensen, Virginia Allen. *Old Mother Hubbard and Her Dog*
Kessler, Leonard. *Kick, Pass, and Run*
Lobel, Arnold. *Frog and Toad Are Friends*
Low, Joseph. *Mice Twice*

CHALLENGING (cont.) ════════════════════

Lundgren, Barbro. *The Wild Baby Goes to Sea*

Parish, Peggy. *Ootah's Lucky Day*

Peet, Bill. *Big Bad Bruce*

Schwartz, Alvin. *There Is a Carrot in My Ear and Other Noodle Tales*

Viorst, Judith. *The Tenth Good Thing about Barney*

AHLBERG, Janet and Allan Ahlberg. *Funnybones.*   Illus. by the authors. Greenwillow, 1980. ISBN: 0-688-84238-0

Big Skeleton, Little Skeleton, and Dog Skeleton set out for a walk in the town. Their purpose is to scare the townspeople. Instead, a strange thing happens to Dog Skeleton while everyone is playing in the park. In the end the plan to scare everyone doesn't work at all. Different animals, along with many big and little skeletons, become involved in the change of plans. In comic-strip format, brightly colored pictures complement the rhythmic language of the text.

Genre: Fantasy

Subject: Skeletons

ALEXANDER, Martha. *We're in Big Trouble, Blackboard Bear.* Illus. by the author. Dial, 1980. ISBN: 0-8037-9742-7

A bear drawn on a blackboard steps out alive. Blackboard Bear did not know how to act in its new environment, but it did know it was hungry. So it ate people's goldfish and berries. Finally, the bear realizes that it shouldn't eat other people's things. Undismayed, Blackboard Bear finds a way to pay people back. Small illustrations in soft shades of blues and reds develop empathy with a bear that is as confused by a new place as young readers might be.

Genre: Fantasy

Subjects: Bears; stealing

ALIKI. *Keep Your Mouth Closed, Dear.* Illus. by the author. Dial, 1966. ISBN: 0-8037-4416-1

Charles the alligator just can't keep his mouth closed. Usually it's not so bad, but every so often Charles swallows terrible things. For example, he swallows a spoon and a clock and a sponge and a can of powder. Nothing his mother can do helps

Charles. He has swallowed so many things that he is beginning to look like a balloon. The climax occurs when he gets his big mouth too close to the vacuum cleaner. The big, green alligators in this family show humanlike reactions to the problem, carrying the comical story to its happy ending.

Genre: Humor
Subjects: Alligators; family life

ALLARD, Harry. *Miss Nelson Is Back.* Illus. by James Marshall. Houghton Mifflin, 1982. ISBN: 0-395-32956-6
Miss Nelson has left the class because they misbehaved, and now the class misses her. Their first substitute was Miss Swamp, and she seemed mean. Now a new substitute will be arriving. The new teacher is full of surprises, and Miss Nelson knows all about them. This is one in a series of books about the popular Miss Nelson.

Genre: Humor
Subjects: Schools, teachers

ALLARD, Harry. *Miss Nelson Is Missing.* Illus. by James Marshall. Houghton Mifflin, 1977. ISBN: 0-395-25296-2
The class was in an unruly mood. The students didn't want to settle down to learn anything and Miss Nelson was unhappy. She was so unhappy that she just quit. Viola Swamp, a mean substitute teacher, took her place. Now the children are sorry they were unruly and want Miss Nelson back. However, no one can find her, not even Detective McSmogy. This is one in a series of books about the adventures of Miss Nelson.

Genre: Humor
Subjects: Schools; teachers; behavior
Award: Georgia Children's Book Award, 1980

ANDERSEN, Hans Christian. *The Princess and the Pea.* Illus. by Paul Galdone. Clarion, 1978. ISBN: 0-395-28807-X
The young woman in this retelling of the Hans Christian Andersen classic appears in the castle and claims to be a princess. Someone needs to decide if she's telling the truth, and the crafty old queen seems to have figured out a way. All she needs are twenty mattresses and one small pea.

Genre: Folklore and fairy tales
Subject: Princesses

ASBJORNSEN, P. C. and J. E. Moe. *The Three Billy Goats Gruff.* Illus. by Marcia Brown. Harcourt, 1987. ISBN: 0-15-286396-6

There's a mean old troll hiding under the bridge and it's waiting to eat the biggest goat. Two goats cross the bridge, but the big one will have to fight that troll. And that's what happens in this classic folk story about a troll who finally meets his match in Big Billy Gruff.

Genre: Folklore and fairy tales
Subjects: Folklore (Norway); goats

ASCH, Frank. *Happy Birthday, Moon.* Illus. by the author. Prentice-Hall, 1982. ISBN: 0-13-383687-8

It is the moon's birthday, or so Bear thinks. Bear must give the moon a birthday present, but what do you give a moon on its birthday? Bear searches everywhere to find a suitable present. It even climbs a mountain before it finds just the right gift! This is one in a series of books about this adventuresome bear.

Genre: Adventure
Subjects: Bears; moon; birthdays

ASCH, Frank. *Moon Bear.* Illus. by the author. Scribner, 1978. ISBN: 0-684-15810-8

Bear is sad because the moon is getting thin. After begging the moon to eat, Bear has an idea. Bear will feed the moon so it can become its normal size again. But Bear doesn't know what moons eat. Bear decides that if bears like honey, then honey must be good for moons too. Now Bear must figure out how to feed the honey to the moon. Line drawings of the bear, the moon, and the stars are framed but extend beyond the frame. The bear is bright, solid brown; the moon and stars are an even brighter solid yellow. Other parts of the illustrations are black and white, emphasizing the characters in the story. This is one in a series of books about this adventuresome bear.

Genre: Adventure
Subjects: Bears; moon

ASCH, Frank. *Mooncake.* Illus. by the author. Prentice-Hall, 1983. ISBN: 0-13-601013-X

In this story silly Bear thinks that the moon is a big cake. To prove that he is right, Bear decides to build a spaceship that could take him to the moon so he can taste it. While Little Bird looks on, Bear starts to make a spaceship. But building a ship is difficult work, and Bear needs to take a rest. However, like all bears, the nap Bear takes lasts into winter. Awakened by noises outside, Bear finds itself in snow and thinks the spaceship has successfully taken the trip. This is one in a series of books about this adventuresome bear.

Genre: Adventure
Subjects: Bears; moon

BABBITT, Natalie. *The Something.* Illus. by the author. Farrar, 1970. ISBN: 0-374-37137-7
Mylo is afraid to sleep. In his dreams, there is something fuzzy in the shadows. Mylo imagines it is some kind of ogre, but he can't make out exactly what it is. He attempts to mold it out of clay so that he can see what the something is. What the clay turns into is a surprise. And the surprise wants a way out of Mylo's dreams just as much as Mylo wants the ogre to let him sleep.

Genre: Realistic fiction
Subjects: Night; dreams; girls

BAKER, Betty. *The Pig War.* Illus. by Robert Lopshire. Harper & Row, 1969. ISBN: 0-06-020333-1
The death of a pig threatens to cause war in this story about an actual incident between the Americans and the British. One army has established a base on an island near Washington. Another country has sent a naval ship to settle the island. The two camps pester each other, as one plays drums and the other blows bugles while they compete for the largest flag. One camp plants gardens and the other raises pigs. The pigs cause the confusion that leads to war. In the end, the two parties decide to live side by side in peace.

Genre: Nonfiction
Subject: U.S. history

BANG, Molly Garrett. *Wiley and the Hairy Man.* Illus. by the author. Macmillan, 1976. ISBN: 0-02-708370-5
Wiley lives with his mother near the swamp where the horrible Hairy Man waits to catch people and eat them. In order for the Hairy Man to stop bothering people, he must be outsmarted by someone three times. However, the Hairy Man is one of the best

conjurers ever. It is up to Wiley to try to outsmart the Hairy Man. Wiley's quick thinking saves him twice when he attempts to fool the Hairy Man—but what will happen the third time? Detailed black-and-white drawings add to the grim, mysterious air of the Hairy Man.

Genre: Folklore and fairy tales
Subjects: Monsters; mothers and sons; cleverness

BEIM, Lorraine and Jerrold Beim. *The Little Igloo.*   Illus. by the authors. Harcourt, 1969. ISBN: 015-246145-7 (o.p.)
Tipou likes to watch his dad build the igloos his people live in. His other favorite pastime is playing with his dog, Kivi. One day, Tipou and Kivi are out playing and roam away from the village. Suddenly a great snowstorm arrives and everything is covered with fresh snow. Tipou is now lost. In the severe arctic weather, he will soon freeze. However, Tipou has watched his father, so he knows how to build a shelter. He builds an igloo, and while inside, Tipou and Kivi keep each other warm until the storm ends and rescuers arrive from the village.

Genre: Realistic fiction
Subjects: Eskimos; boys; dogs; families

BEMELMANS, Ludwig. *Madeleine.*   Illus. by the author. Viking, 1939. ISBN: 0-670-44580-0
Twelve girls live in a boarding school and all sleep in the same room. At night they chatter until their teacher turns out the lights, and then all becomes quiet. One night, Madeleine begins to cry because her stomach hurts. She is rushed to the hospital to have her appendix removed. All goes well, and soon her 11 roommates come to visit her. The girls are impressed with the hospital, so impressed that that night all 11 of them begin to cry. Simple rhyming narrative makes the story easy to read. This is one in a series of books about Madeleine.

Genre: Realistic fiction
Subjects: Girls; illness

BENCHLEY, Nathaniel. *George the Drummer Boy.*   Illus. by Don Bolognese. Harper & Row, 1977. ISBN: 0-06-020500-8
It is 1776, and the American colonists have decided to be free from England. With the outbreak of fighting near Boston, the

war begins. Eventually, the Americans are victorious and their side of the story is told. But what about the defeated British army, thousands of miles from home? George is a drummer boy for the English. This is his story.

Genre: Historical fiction
Subjects: Battle of Lexington, 1775; Battle of Concord, 1775

BENCHLEY, Nathaniel. *The Strange Disappearance of Arthur Cluck.*   Illus. by Arnold Lobel. Harper & Row, 1967. ISBN: 0-06-020478-8
Old Owl needs to find a missing chick, Arthur. But how can the owl find Arthur among all the little, fuzzy, yellow chicks? It's easy if you know Arthur's one crazy way of acting.

Genre: Mystery
Subjects: Owls; chickens

BLAINE, Marge. *The Terrible Thing That Happened at Our House.*   Illus. by John C. Wallner. Four Winds, 1980. ISBN: 0-590-07780-5
A family consisting of mother, father, son, and daughter is used to having the mother do everything around the house. The daughter tells the story of what happens when the mother gets a job. At first it is terrible. Nothing ever gets done at home. But, finally, the family finds a way to adjust to a working mother.

Genre: Realistic fiction
Subjects: Family life; mother's employment

BLUME, Judy. *The Pain and the Great One.*   Illus. by Irene Trivas. Bradbury, 1984. ISBN: 0-02-711100-8
Everyone has moments when it seems better to be someone else. A girl has a baby brother who gets all the attention. She would like to share the spotlight with her brother, the Pain. On the other hand, she would like to be able to swim and make things like her older sister, the Great One. In the end, though, the girl decides that it's better to be oneself.

Genre: Realistic fiction
Subject: Brothers and sisters

BOND, Felicia. *Poinsettia and the Firefighters.*   Illus. by the author. Crowell, 1984. ISBN: 0-690-04401-1

Poinsettia the pig was lonely and afraid of the dark in her new room. The noises outside were so frightening that she could not sleep. One sleepless night Poinsettia notices fire and this leads to the discovery that not everyone sleeps when it's dark. The firefighters are awake and that changes everything, especiallv the way Poinsettia feels. This is one in a series about Poinsettia's feelings and adventures.

Genre: Realistic fiction
Subjects: Pigs; night; fear; firefighters

BONSALL, Crosby Newell. *Tell Me Some More.*   Illus. by Fritz Siebel. Harper & Row, 1961. ISBN: 0-06-020601-2
There is only one place in the world where you can find how it feels to hold an elephant, pat a lion, or tickle a seal. And these are only a few of the things you can do in this amazing place. Andrew tells Tim, and Tim wants to hear more. It's not the circus or the zoo. What could it be?

Genre: Realistic fiction
Subject: Libraries

BRANDENBERG, Franz. *Leo and Emily's Big Ideas.*   Illus. by Aliki. Greenwillow, 1982. ISBN: 0-688-00755-4
In three stories, Leo and Emily search for a good idea. The first idea, to scare everyone, only works on Leo. The second idea, to play in Emily's imaginary toolshed, gets them all wet. A flag for their shed is the third idea. They find that 100 flags can be bought for ten dollars and they can sell the extra ones. This big idea leads to the problem of what to do with 31 extra flags. This is one in a series of books about the adventures of Leo and Emily.

Genre: Adventure
Subject: Friendship

BRANDENBERG, Franz. *Nice New Neighbors.*   Illus. by Aliki. Greenwillow, 1977. ISBN: 0-688-84105-8
A large field mouse family with many children—Annette, Bertrand, Colette, Daniel, Esther, and Ferdinand—has just moved into a new community. They wonder what to do in a new town where no one wants to play with them. It isn't easy to win new friends, especially if you are a mouse. But these mice are smart, and they come up with the perfect plan. Pinks and greens

enliven the black and white in the drawings. This is one in a series of books about this large and lively field mouse family.

Genre: Realistic fiction
Subjects: Mice; friendship

BROWN, Margaret Wise. *Runaway Bunny.* Illus. by Clement Hurd. Harper & Row, 1972. ISBN: 06-020765-5
The little rabbit is upset with his mother and tells her how he plans to run away from home. The little rabbit has everything planned. But for every part of the plan, his mother has more than one way to catch the little runner. Small black-and-white drawings mix with brightly colored ones to help young readers sort the little rabbit's ideas from his mother's.

Genre: Realistic fiction
Subjects: Rabbits; family life; runaways

BURNINGHAM, John. *Come Away from the Water, Shirley.* Illus. by the author. Crowell, 1977. ISBN: 0-690-01360-4
Shirley and her parents are at the beach. But it's not much fun because her mother wants Shirley to stay away from the water. Shirley will obey her mother, but she can still imagine being on a pirate ship. While on this ship, Shirley is fighting for the fantastic treasures that are aboard. Contrasting drawings on right- and left-hand pages help readers distinguish between the reality of the family and the fantasy of Shirley's imagination. Sketchy drawings accompany the mother's narrative; large, brightly colored, fanciful drawings on the facing pages illustrate Shirley's dream of pirates and ships. This is one in a series of books about Shirley and the way she behaves.

Genre: Realistic fiction
Subjects: Imagination; seashore; pirates
Award: *New York Times* Best Illustrated Children's Books of the Year, 1977

BURNINGHAM, John. *Mr. Gumpy's Motor Car.* Illus. by the author. Crowell, 1976. ISBN: 0-690-00799-X
Mr. Gumpy has a new car and is about to take it for a spin in the country. Of course the children want to go along, as do the rabbit, cat, dog, pig, chicken, calf, and goat. Everyone piles into the car. It is a nice day at first, but then it starts to rain. Soon the car

is bogged down in the mud and everyone is pushing and shouting to get it moving again. Finally, the car jumps forward and is filled again with mud-covered people and animals. It is not the best of rides until Mr. Gumpy finds a way to get everyone clean and end the day on a happy note. This is one book in a series about the adventures of Mr. Gumpy.

Genre: Adventure
Subjects: Families; cars; storms

BURNINGHAM, John. *Mr. Gumpy's Outing.* Illus. by the author. Holt, 1970. ISBN: 0-03-089733-5
Mr. Gumpy lives by a river and has a boat. He likes to go out in his boat by himself. But today the children want to go, and so do their animal friends. One by one they ask and Mr. Gumpy agrees, if they behave as he says. Finally, with everyone on the small boat, they get underway. But the guests don't behave as Mr. Gumpy says, so naturally the vessel meets with mishap before bringing its passengers back home again. This is one book in a series about Mr. Gumpy.

Genre: Humor
Subjects: Boats and boating; animals; behavior
Awards: *Boston Globe-Horn* Book Awards (illustration), 1972; *New York Times* Best Illustrated Children's Books of the Year, 1971; Kate Greenaway Medal, 1970

BURNINGHAM, John. *The Shopping Basket.* Illus. by the author. Crowell, 1980. ISBN: 0-690-04083-0
Steven's mother sends him to the market to get six eggs, five bananas, four apples, three oranges. . . . On the way home, he meets, one after another, some very strange and unfriendly characters. On his way home he loses some of the items his mother sends him for. She'll never believe how they got lost.

Genre: Humor
Subjects: Animals; cleverness

CALHOUN, Mary. *Cross-Country Cat.* Illus. by Erick Ingraham. Morrow, 1979. ISBN: 0-688-22186-6
Henry the cat is a smart cat, but he doesn't like snow at all. He certainly doesn't want to learn to ski when his owners take him on a trip. But when the family drives off without him, Henry has

no choice. He makes some skis and sets off toward home. Henry learns to ski while escaping a dangerous situation. Eventually, this resourceful cat is rescued by his family, who have come back to find him. This is one in a series of books about the adventures of Henry.

Genre: Fantasy
Subjects: Cats; cross-country skiing
Awards: Wisconsin Little Archer Award, 1980; Colorado Children's Book Award, 1981; Washington Children's Choice Picture Book Award, 1982

CALHOUN, Mary. *Hot Air Henry.* Illus. by Erick Ingraham. Morrow, 1981. ISBN: 0-688-04068-3
Kid, Man, and Woman are preparing to fly a hot air balloon. They fill the balloon with air and put the hot air fan in place. Then, just before the trio sets off, leaving the cat, Henry, behind, each flyer has to leave the balloon to do a last-minute chore. Curious, Henry takes the opportunity to explore the balloon and accidentally trips the mooring line. The balloon soars into the air with Henry searching for a way to bring it down. His adventure leads to an encounter with an eagle, a scare when his balloon meets a flock of geese, and bumpy landings before a rescue by the anxious family. This is one in a series of books about the adventures of Henry.

Genre: Adventure
Subjects: Balloons; cats

CHAPMAN, Carol. *The Tale of Meshka the Kvetch.* Illus. by Arnold Lobel. Dutton, 1980. ISBN: 0-525-40745-6
Kvetch is the Yiddish word for "complainer," and Meshka is a real kvetch. Finally, there are consequences to her constant complaints. When Meshka grumbles about this or that her words become reality, as when she complains about tired feet that feel like melons and her feet become melons. It's magic. Meshka has to change before this story can end happily.

Genre: Humor
Subjects: Behavior; conduct of life

COERR, Eleanor. *The Big Balloon Race.* Illus. by Carolyn Croll. Harper & Row, 1981. ISBN 0-06-021352-3

This is an adventure tale that opens with Ariel, who has never ridden in a balloon before, being allowed to sit in a balloon basket while her mother prepares for the big balloon race. When the balloon inadvertently sets sail, Ariel's added weight creates some problems for her mother and wild adventures for Ariel. Brightly colored balloons background the comical but serious illustrations of Ariel's predicaments as she and her mother struggle to keep the balloon in proper balance. The story is based on the lives of a famous pioneering balloonist family.

Genre: Adventure
Subjects: Girls; balloons; mothers

DABCOVICH, Lydia. *Follow the River.*   Illus. by the author. Dutton, 1980. ISBN: 0-525-30015-5
The river is big and wide, yet it wasn't always that way. By following the river in this book, the reader sees where it comes from and where it goes. As the river moves from the mountains to the sea, the reader will also see that bridges cross it, rain falls on it, sun warms it, and living things use it.

Genre: Concept books
Subject: Rivers

DELTON, Judy. *Two Good Friends.*   Illus. by Giulio Maestro. Crown, 1974. ISBN: 0-517-55949-8
This story is about two friends, Tidy Duck and Messy Bear, who are opposites. One is messy and the other is neat. Messy Bear can cook and Tidy Duck can't. Despite their differences, the two friends are inseparable and find a way to get along. This is one in a series of books about the two friends.

Genre: Realistic fiction
Subjects: Friendship; animals

dePAOLA, Tomie. *Things to Make and Do for Valentine's Day.*
Illus. by the author. Franklin Watts, 1976. ISBN: 0-531-01187-9
By following the directions in this book, readers can make all kinds of things for their friends on Valentine's Day. Recipes, games, cards—these are just some of the ideas in this information-packed book. There are even valentines jokes to add to the fun. The renowned author-illustrator uses comic-book style pictures that are a source for much of the information.

Genre: Nonfiction
Subjects: Holidays (Valentine's Day); handicrafts

dePAOLA, Tomie. *Watch Out for the Chicken Feet in Your Soup.* Illus. by the author. Prentice-Hall, 1974. ISBN: 0-13-945782-8
This true-to-life tale is about Joey's grandmother. She is Italian, has a foreign accent, and cooks soup with chicken feet in it. Although her differences make Joey feel uncomfortable, he brings his friend Eugene over to dinner. Is he surprised when his friend eats everything, including the soup with the chicken feet! The story shows the reader that there's nothing wrong with differences—they might even be interesting.
Genre: Realistic fiction
Subjects: Grandmothers; Italians (United States)

De REGNIERS, Beatrice Schenk. *Red Riding Hood.* Illus. by Edward Gorey. Macmillan, 1977. ISBN: 0-689-70435-6
This is a retelling of the old fairy tale in verse. Once again there is a mean wolf. He's going to eat Red Riding Hood and her sick old grandmother. That's the wolf's plan, but the woodsman has a plan of his own.
Genre: Folklore and fairy tales
Subjects: Wolves; folklore (Germany); stories in rhyme

DUVOISIN, Roger. *Petunia.* Illus. by the author. Knopf, 1950. ISBN: 0-394-90865-1
Petunia the goose thinks she can get smart just by carrying a book under her wing. She thinks she's so smart that she can give advice to everyone. However, there's a slight problem, because her advice is not very wise. Thinking she is smart causes trouble for everyone but Petunia. In the end the not-so-silly goose discovers that only by reading the book will she become wise. This is one in a series of books about this comical heroine.
Genre: Humor
Subject: Geese

GACKENBACH, Dick. *Harry and the Terrible Whatzit.* Illus. by the author. Clarion, 1978. ISBN: 0-395-28795-20
In this fantasy, Harry is certain there's a monster in the basement. It's a big, threatening beast with two heads. Harry's mother is down there, and he wants to do something to help her. What he finally does helps him conquer his own fear and changes the monster into a beast that is not so terrible after all.

The story finishes humorously, although there's a scream, not laughter, from the house next door.

Genre: Fantasy
Subjects: Fear; mothers and sons

GAGE, Wilson. *Squash Pie.* Illus. by Glen Rounds. Greenwillow, 1976. ISBN: 0-688-80031-9 (o.p.)
In this funny mystery, a farmer likes squash pie. But someone else doesn't. So every time a squash is nearly ready to harvest, the farmer finds it stolen or smashed. By carefully reading the pictures and text, the reader unlocks the identity of the mysterious squash thief. However, the culprit has never tried squash pie, so how can she hate it so much? Then, one day, she takes a taste, and everything changes for the better.

Genre: Humor
Subjects: Gardening; robbers and outlaws; squash

GALDONE, Paul. *The Gingerbread Boy.* Illus. by the author. Clarion, 1975. ISBN: 0-395-28799-5
This is a retelling of the classic fairy tale. A little old lady has made a wonderful gingerbread boy, but she has made him too well. He jumps from the pan and runs through the countryside. The gingerbread boy can run so fast that no one can catch it — except perhaps that fox.

Genre: Folklore and fairy tales
Subject: Animals

GALDONE, Paul. *The Three Little Pigs.* Illus. by the author. Clarion, 1970. ISBN: 0-395-28813-4
In this retelling of Joseph Jacobs folktale, the reader sees a wolf that looks mean — and it is. The three little pigs go off into the world to seek their fortune, which turns into misfortune for two of them. Their weak houses cannot withstand the hungry wolf, but the third brother's house is different. That third one is a smart pig; he's built a house of bricks and is ready for the wolf when it tries to come down the chimney. Perhaps the wolf will now make a good dinner for someone.

Genre: Folklore and fairy tales
Subjects: Pigs; wolves; folklore

GINSBURG, Mirra. *Good Morning, Chick.* Illus. by Byron Barton. Greenwillow, 1980. ISBN: 0-688-80284-2
When the little chick breaks out of its egg, it can already do many things. However, there's still a great deal it has to learn from its mother, like how to eat worms, and life is a constant adventure. Being scared by a cat and falling into a pond are two of the incidents that happen to the newborn.

Genre: Concept book
Subject: Chickens

HAMILTON, Morse and Emily Hamilton. *My Name Is Emily.* Illus. by Jenni Oliver. Greenwillow, 1979. ISBN: 0-688-80181-1 (o.p.)
A five-year-old girl decides to run away from home, then changes her mind. When she returns, her father plays a trick on her. Yes, the girl has brown hair and gray eyes, and she's exactly the same size and has the same name as the man's daughter. She, too, has a baby sister named Kate who is taking up a lot of her parents' time. But this man's older daughter ran away from home, so who can this girl be?

Genre: Realistic fiction
Subjects: Fathers and daughters; family life

HOBAN, Russell. *A Bargain for Frances.* Illus. by Lillian Hoban. Harper & Row, 1970. ISBN: 0-06-022329-4
Frances the badger thought Thelma was her friend, but Frances's mother warned her to be careful. Whenever the two played together, Thelma seemed to get the best of Frances. This time Thelma tricks Frances into making a poor bargain: Frances's carefully saved money for Thelma's old tea set. Frances will not be outsmarted, though. In the end she gets the best of Thelma, and chances are Thelma will think twice before tricking Frances again. This is one in a series of books about Frances, the childlike badger.

Genre: Realistic fiction
Subjects: Badgers; friendship

HOBAN, Russell. *Dinner at Alberta's.* Illus. by James Marshall. Crowell, 1975. ISBN: 0-690-23993-9

Bad table manners! That is just what you would expect from a crocodile. Arthur will have to learn fast if he is going to have a good time at Alberta's when he goes there for dinner. For a week Arthur takes lessons. Emma helps, but some of the lessons don't work out so well. Still, everyone manages to have a good time at Alberta's, even Arthur.

Genre: Humor
Subjects: Etiquette; crocodiles

HOBAN, Russell. *Nothing to Do.* Illus. by Lillian Hoban. Harper & Row, 1964. ISBN: 0-06-022390-1
Walter the opossum never seemed to have anything to do. Then his father gave him a magic stone. All Walter has to do is keep it nearby and he will never be bored. How can a stone be something to do? Well, it works just as well as his sister Charlotte's magic stick.

Genre: Humor
Subject: Opossums

HOFF, Syd. *Danny and the Dinosaur.* Illus. by the author. Harper & Row, 1958. ISBN: 0-06-022465-7
The dinosaur that Danny sees in the museum is no ordinary replica. This dinosaur comes alive and shows Danny a great time. The boy rides the reptile through town and the dinosaur acts like a bridge so people can cross the street. The dinosaur visits the zoo and is quite a hit at a baseball game. It even plays hide-and-seek with Danny's friends—and that's quite a trick for a dinosaur as huge as this one.

Genre: Fantasy
Subject: Dinosaurs

HUTCHINS, Pat. *You'll Soon Grow into Them, Titch.* Illus. by the author. Greenwillow, 1982. ISBN: 0-688-01770-3
Titch has an older brother and sister. He is always getting hand-me-downs to wear, and they never quite fit. But he always hears the same phrase—he'll soon grow into them. Titch is not sure he likes being the one who wears these old clothes. But everything changes when the new baby comes. Now Titch will be able to hand his clothes down to someone and can assure the baby of growing into them. This is one in a series of books about Titch.

Genre: Realistic fiction
Subjects: Brothers and sisters; clothing and dress

JENSEN, Virginia Allen. *Old Mother Hubbard and Her Dog.* Trans. by Lennart Hellsing. Illus. by Ib Spang Olsen. Coward, 1976. ISBN: 0-698-20348-8 (o.p.)
Every time Mother Hubbard leaves the dog, it does something crazy. She tries everything to control the dog, but she can't seem to make him behave. One day, Mother Hubbard went to the tailor's to buy the dog a coat, and when she came back he was riding a goat. And that is only one example of the dog's silly antics. Each is humorously described in this Swedish version of the Mother Goose rhyme.
Genre: Folklore and fairy tales
Subjects: Dogs; stories in rhyme; folklore

JONAS, Ann. *The Quilt.* Illus. by the author. Greenwillow, 1984. ISBN: 0-688-03825-5
The girl in this story gets a new patchwork quilt made by her parents. The pieces in the patchwork are parts of her past—her baby pajamas, a forgotten pair of pants, her old stuffed dog Sally. Later, in a dream about Sally, the patches in the quilt are magically transformed into a dream world where she searches for her pet. Detailed illustrations in a range of colors provide a great deal to "read" along with the text.
Genre: Realistic fiction
Subjects: Quilts; bedtime; families

KEATS, Ezra Jack. *Dreams.* Illus. by the author. Macmillan, 1974. ISBN: 0-02-749610-4
Everyone was dreaming except Roberto. One night he was lying in bed with a paper mouse. Roberto got up and went to the window and accidentally knocked the paper mouse into the air. As the mouse floated to earth he saw it scare away a big dog and thus a cat was saved. The night is vividly captured in pictures colored with bright oranges, blues, reds, and greens.
Genre: Realistic fiction
Subjects: Animals; toys

KEATS, Ezra Jack. *The Snowy Day.* Illus. by the author. Viking, 1962. ISBN: 0-670-65400-0
Snowy days are great fun! Peter is having a fine time—making tracks in the fresh-fallen whiteness, listening to the crunch of his feet in the powder, making a smiling snowman, and sliding

down a mountain of snow. A pile of snow falls on him, too, but such inconveniences hardly matter on this joyfully white day. This is one in a series of books about Peter and his experiences.

Genre: Realistic fiction
Subject: Snow
Award: Caldecott Medal Honor Books, 1963

KELLER, Holly. *Geraldine's Blanket.* Illus. by the author. Greenwillow, 1984. ISBN: 0-688-02539-0
In this near-to-life story, the reader can associate with Geraldine's problem—it's hard to give up a thing even when it's old. This is how it is with Geraldine's pink blanket. It has grown old and worn until there is only a small piece left. But even then, the resourceful little girl finds a clever way to use it.

Genre: Realistic fiction
Subjects: Blankets; families

KELLOGG, Steven. *The Mystery of the Missing Red Mitten.* Illus. by the author. Dial, 1974. ISBN: 0-8037-6194-5
It's easy to lose things in the snow—a gray boot, a white scarf, a brown sweater. But how could anyone possibly lose a red mitten? Annie and Oscar the dog look everywhere, but it's a mystery that only the snowman can solve. Small delicate drawings in black and white reveal where the search will end, as the mitten appears in bright red.

Genre: Mystery
Subject: Losing things

KELLOGG, Steven. *The Mystery of the Stolen Blue Paint.* Illus. by the author. Dial, 1982. ISBN: 0-6037-5654-2
Belinda is trying very hard to paint a blue picture for her room but something keeps getting in the way. Then, as if all the trouble Belinda's been having isn't enough, the blue paint disappears. She suspects the small children, then feels ashamed when her dog starts kissing everyone and the mystery is solved.

Genre: Mystery
Subject: Losing things

KESSLER, Leonard. *Kick, Pass, and Run.* Illus. by the author. Harper & Row, 1966. ISBN: 0-06-023159-9

The animals of the forest find a football and are bent on learning how to play. Being rabbits, ducks, and other forest animals, they do not know the rules of the game. But they decide to try to play. It turns out to be unusual in that one of the birds seems to think it's fair to fly with the ball. This comical story provides information on football positions, rules, and words.

Genre: Humor
Subjects: Animals; football

KRASILOVSKY, Phyllis. *The Man Who Entered a Contest.* Illus. by Yuri Salzman. Doubleday, 1980. ISBN: 0-385-13351-0
The stove was very old, but the man entered the contest anyway. He was going to bake his last cake in the old stove. However, disaster strikes — the cat knocks over the baking batter, and then the cake starts to overflow everywhere. Now the man has a cake chair, a cake stove, a cake kitchen — and the judges are about to arrive to evaluate his entry in the contest.

Genre: Humor
Subject: Cookery

KROLL, Steven. *One Tough Turkey.* Illus. by John Wallner. Holiday House, 1982. ISBN: 0-8234-0457-9
It's Thanksgiving and the Pilgrims want turkey for dinner. Captain Bill Fitz and company are out to hunt them, and the family of turkeys — Solomon, Lavinia, Regina, and Alfred — is likely to be eaten. But Solomon, the father in this turkey family, has other ideas and in his own funny way manages to fool the hunters.

Genre: Humor
Subjects: Holidays (Thanksgiving Day); turkeys

LEAF, Munro. *The Story of Ferdinand.* Illus. by Robert Lawson. Viking, 1936. ISBN: 0-670-67424-9
Ferdinand seems awfully strange for a bull. He's strong and big enough, but he likes to sit and smell the flowers instead of fighting. Then, one day, he sits on a bee and goes so wild that he seems ferocious. The men from the bullring have come to look for a bull for the fight and it's easy to imagine who they choose.

Genre: Humor
Subjects: Bulls; bullfights

LOBEL, Arnold. *Frog and Toad Are Friends.*   Illus. by the author. Harper & Row, 1970. ISBN: 0-06-023957-3
A frog and a toad are friends in the five stories told in this book. In one story, Frog is sick and Toad tries to make him feel better; in another, Toad goes swimming and all the animals, even Frog, laugh at his bathing suit. The stories are related in theme—each is about what it's like to have a good friend—and there is a quiet warmth to them all. This is one in a series of books about Frog and Toad.

Genre: Humor
Subjects: Frogs; friendships; toads
Awards: Caldecott Medal Honor Books, 1971; Finalist in National Book Awards, 1971

LOBEL, Arnold. *A Treeful of Pigs.* Illus. by Anita Lobel. Greenwillow, 1979. ISBN: 0-688-80177-3
A lazy farmer wanted pigs, and promised his wife that he would help to take care of the pigs, but now he won't take care of them. In a sarcastic manner, he says that he'll help when pigs grow on trees. And sure enough one morning he finds them up in a tree. However, the trick doesn't get him to change his ways, and neither does anything else until his wife comes up with the answer.

Genre: Humor
Subjects: Laziness; pigs; farm life

LOCKER, Thomas. *The Mare on the Hill.*   Illus. by the author. Dial, 1985. ISBN: 0-8037-0207-8
A father brings home a white mare that has been treated cruelly by its last owner. The horse becomes frightened when it comes into contact with humans. So it is not surprising that for a full year the mare refuses to let the boys come near. When winter arrives, they carry food to the mare, but still the frightened horse will not be their friend. Then spring arrives and there is a special surprise for the farm family. Richly colored illustrations capture nature's changes from season to season.

Genre: Realistic fiction
Subject: Horses

LOW, Joseph. *Mice Twice.*   Illus. by the author. Atheneum, 1980. ISBN: 0-689-50157-9

A cat has invited a mouse to dinner, with ulterior motives. The cat has plans for a mouse dinner, but the mouse has plans too. It asks if it can bring along a friend. Thus the cat looks forward to a two-mouse dinner, but its plans go astray when the friend turns out to be a dog.

Genre: Humor
Subject: Animals
Awards: Caldecott Medal Honor Books, 1981; ALA Notable Children's Books, 1980

LUNDGREN, Barbro. *The Wild Baby Goes to Sea.* Adapted from the Swedish story by Jack Prelutsky. Illus. by Eva Eriksson. Greenwillow, 1983. ISBN: 0-688-01960-8
This story is about Ben, who wants an adventure. He makes a boat from a box and uses his mother's apron for a sail. Then, in his imagination, he sets sail, after first inviting Mouse, Giraffe, and Bunny to sail with him. From then on it's one adventurous moment after another: Mouse falls into the sea, a hungry fish threatens them, they save a drowning rooster, and sail inside a whale. The rhythmic language of the story should hold the reader's interest.

Genre: Adventure
Subjects: Imagination; stories in rhyme

McPHAIL, David. *The Train.* Illus. by the author. Little, Brown, 1977. ISBN: 0-316-56316-1
In this story, Matthew's train is broken and he sets out to fix it. He manages to get the train working again but then falls asleep. In his dream Matthew is the conductor of a real train—greeting passengers, punching tickets, and loading baggage. The story tells of a wonderful experience inspired by the toy train.

Genre: Realistic fiction
Subjects: Boys; toys (trains)

MAHY, Margaret. *The Boy Who Was Followed Home.* Illus. by Steven Kellogg. Dial, 1975. ISBN: 0-8037-0286-8
Robert doesn't know why that hippo followed him home from school. But every day the hippo seems to bring along more of its hippo friends. They certainly will have to leave because everything is becoming crowded. They're filling up the fish pond,

then the whole yard. A witch in town knows how to get rid of the hippos—but she forgot to tell Robert about the side effects of her magic pill. The hippos are now gone but they've been replaced. The openness and humorous expressions on the faces of the animals make the illustrations an important part in the telling of this story.

Genre: Fantasy
Subjects: Hippopotamuses; witches

MARSHALL, Edward. *Troll Country.*   Illus. by James Marshall. Dial, 1980. ISBN: 0-8037-6211-9
Elsie hears her mother explain how she escaped from a troll. And sure enough, it's Elsie's luck to meet the very same troll. She's prepared, though; she knows about the troll and soon finds a way of her own to escape.

Genre: Fantasy
Subjects: Trolls; girls

MODELL, Frank. *Seen Any Cats?*   Illus. by the author. Greenwillow, 1979. ISBN: 0-688-80229-X
Milton and Marvin have a great idea for earning money to go to the circus. All they need is some cats to train for a show. Milton finds plenty of cats, and the boys set out to train them. But the cats have other ideas. Just when the boys are ready to present their cat show, all the cats run away.

Genre: Realistic fiction
Subjects: Boys; cats

MORRIS, Robert A. *Seahorse.*   Illus. by Arnold Lobel. Harper & Row, 1972. ISBN: 0-06-024339-2
The seahorse is such a tiny creature that it is hard to imagine how it escapes from bigger fish and survives ocean storms. In this realistic story, the life of one of the sea's most unusual animals is traced. It describes what the seahorse eats, where it lives, and how it reproduces. The detailed drawings show the seahorse in various circumstances, for example, hiding in the seaweed forest.

Genre: Nonfiction
Subject: Seahorses

NAKATANI, Chiyoko. *The Zoo in My Garden.* Illus. by the author. Crowell, 1973. ISBN: 0-690-95904-4 (o.p.)
In this story a boy watches the animals in his garden closely. The animals include dogs, sparrows, pigeons, snails, and butterflies. Large, brightly colored watercolor drawings show the beauty of the "zoo" in the garden.

Genre: Realistic fiction
Subject: Gardens

NOBLE, Trinka Hakes. *The Day Jimmy's Boa Ate the Wash.* Illus. by Steven Kellogg. Dial, 1980. ISBN: 0-8037-1723-7
It might have been a dull field trip to a farm if Jimmy's pet boa hadn't come along. But the playful boa scared the chickens, causing one of them to lay an egg on Jenny' s head. And to top it off, the boa got tangled in the farmer's wife's wash. Things became so mixed up that Jimmy wound up with another kind of pet. This is one of a series of books about Jimmy's boa constrictor.

Genre: Humor
Subjects: Boa constrictor; snakes; farms; schools; pets

NOBLE, Trinka Hakes. *Jimmy's Boa Bounces Back.* Illus. by Steven Kellogg. Dial, 1984. ISBN: 0-8037-0050-4
The same pet boa that caused so much trouble on the field trip to a farm in an earlier book has gotten into trouble again and is sent home — just in time. Jimmy's mother is going to a club party and needs something to wear. With the boa as part of her outfit, Jimmy's mother is a sensation until the snake moves. This starts a chain reaction that disrupts the party and ends with the boa as a hero for having rescued a puppy from the punch. This is one in a series of books about Jimmy's boa constrictor.

Genre: Humor
Subjects: Boa constrictor; snakes; pets

NØDSET, Joan L. *Come Here, Cat.* Illus. by Steven Kellogg. Harper & Row, 1973. ISBN: 0-06-024558-1
The girl in this story finds out what can happen when you chase a cat. All the girl is trying to do is pet the cat and make friends

with it. It continually escapes her until she stops chasing it and sits down.

Genre: Realistic fiction
Subjects: Cats; pets

PARISH, Peggy. *Amelia Bedelia Helps Out.* Illus. by Lynn Sweat. Greenwillow, 1963. ISBN: 0-688-80231-1
Amelia Bedelia is about the funniest housekeeper anyone could ever hope to meet. She acts on the literal meaning of people's words. For example, when her instructions are to "dust the bugs," she figures this means it's time to clean the pesky little beasts. Every instruction has a word that's misinterpreted by the unusual maid. This is one in a series of books about Amelia Bedelia and the comical situations her actions inspire.

Genre: Humor
Subject: Vocabulary

PARISH, Peggy. *Ootah's Lucky Day.* Illus. by Namoru Funai. Harper & Row, 1970. ISBN: 0-06-024645-6
Ootah lives in an Eskimo village. It's now the season when the villagers hunt walrus for food. All the men and older boys of the village help in the hunt, but everyone thinks Ootah is too small for the walrus hunting. Left to fend for himself, Ootah finds a walrus and is able to kill it to add to the village food supply.

Genre: Realistic fiction
Subjects: Eskimos; hunting; walrus

PEET, Bill. *Big Bad Bruce.* Illus. by the author. Houghton Mifflin, 1977. ISBN: 0-395-25150-8
Big Bad Bruce is a bear that loves to roll rocks into people. His misbehavior is not appreciated, but he is too big to be challenged by anyone except the witch. After she's done with him, he's no longer "Big" but he still appears to be "Bad."

Genre: Fantasy
Subjects: Bears; witches
Awards: Georgia Children's Book Award, 1979; California Young Readers' Medal, 1981

PRESTON, Edna Mitchell. *Squawk to the Moon, Little Goose.* Illus. by Barbara Cooney. Viking, 1985. ISBN: 0-14-050546-6

Little Goose thinks a fox is eating the moon, so it squawks and wakes the farmer. Then Little Goose sees the moon reflected in a pond and thinks it has fallen, so she wakes the farmer again. Finally, she has a real problem—she's caught by a fox. This time, though, when she squawks, the farmer won't help, and Little Goose is left to fend for herself in this modern-day fable.

Genre: Folklore and fairy tales
Subjects: Geese; foxes; moon

QUIN-HARKIN, Janet. *Helpful Hattie.* Illus. by Susanna Natti. Harcourt, 1983. ISBN: 0-152-33756-3
Hattie is always trying to help. In this funny story, the reader sees some of the predicaments she gets herself into. For example, she decides to help her busy mother frost a birthday cake. Edward, her new friend who is coming to help eat the cake, had better like catsup frosting. Then Hattie tries to save money by cutting her own hair. Now she looks like a toothbrush. What trouble will Helpful Hattie get into next?

Genre: Humor
Subjects: Birthdays; haircutting; teeth; helpfulness

REY, H. A. and Margaret Rey (in collaboration with the Children's Hospital Medical Center). *Curious George Goes to the Hospital.* Illus. by the authors. Houghton Mifflin, 1966. ISBN: 0-395-18158-5
George the monkey has a stomachache. He found a box and opened it. The contents looked so pretty that George had to eat one. His curiosity lands him in a hospital and he finds that a hospital is no place for a monkey. However, George becomes a hero when he makes a girl in the hospital smile. This book is one in a series about Curious George.

Genre: Adventure
Subjects: Monkeys; hospitals
Award: Child Study Children's Book Committee at Bank Street College Special Citation, 1966

RICE, Eve. *Benny Bakes a Cake.* Illus. by the author. Greenwillow, 1981. ISBN: 0-688-80312-1
In this real-life situation story it is Benny's birthday. Benny has helped his mother bake the cake, but his dog, Ralph, gets in the

way. The cake and the birthday will be a disaster unless Benny's father can find a way to fix everything.

Genre: Realistic fiction
Subjects: Birthdays; cake

ROCKWELL, Anne. *Poor Goose.*   Illus. by the author. Crowell, 1976. ISBN: 0-690-01014-1 (o.p.)
Poor Goose has a headache and everyone feels sorry for the animal. The cat, turtle, cow, and even the little old lady would like to help, but the real problem isn't a headache. By the end of the story all the animals know what Goose's real trouble is. The pages in this book are busy with words on top of geometric patterns that border the illustrations.

Genre: Folklore and fairy tales
Subjects: Animals; folklore (France)

SCHWARTZ, Alvin. *There Is a Carrot in My Ear and Other Noodle Tales.*   Illus. by Karen Ann Weinhaus. Harper & Row, 1982. ISBN: 0-06-025233-2
A member of the family has a carrot in its ear. It seems that that's not unusual for these silly people. In these six stories about the Noodlehead family everyone does something strange. These tales are retellings of older stories and each features antics as silly as using a ruler to discover how long a person sleeps.

Genre: Folklore and fairy tales
Subject: Wit and humor

SENDAK, Maurice. *In the Night Kitchen.*   Illus. by the author. Harper & Row, 1970. ISBN: 0-06-025489-0
In this story, a boy is asleep in the dark and dreams that he is on a wild journey. He flies through the air and lands in his own kitchen where cooks are at work using gigantic pots. The boy tumbles right into the cake batter that is just ready for baking. He escapes by shaping an airplane from bread dough and flying over the Milky Way. The wildly exciting illustrations add to the excitement of this dream journey.

Genre: Fantasy
Subjects: Boys; dreams

SHARMAT, Marjorie Weinman. *Griselda's New Year.*   Illus. by Normand Chartier. Macmillan, 1979. ISBN: 0-02-782420-9

Griselda the goose makes a New Year resolution. All she wants to do is to be good and make someone happy. However, the silly goose is blissfully unaware of all the trouble she causes for Brutus Lion, Morgan Goat, and Desdemona Dog. Griselda winds up with goose bumps, a lump on her head, and a blue foot. But in her own silly way, she fixes these troubles and settles in for a Happy New Year.

Genre: Humor
Subjects: Geese; holidays (New Year)

SHARMAT, Marjorie Weinman. *Nate the Great and the Missing Key.* Illus. by Marc Simont. Coward, 1981. ISBN: 0-698-30726-7

Nate, the great detective, likes Annie a lot. But he has a different feeling toward her mean dog. Nate's problem is that Annie wants to have a birthday party for her dog. However, a mystery develops because Annie has lost her house key and she can't have the party until she finds it. Nate now has a dilemma: If he finds the key, he'll have to go to the mean dog's party. This is one in a series of books about the cases solved by Nate.

Genre: Mystery
Subject: Finding things
Award: Garden State Children's Book Award, 1984

SHARMAT, Marjorie Weinman. *Nate the Great and the Snowy Trail.* Illus. by Marc Simont. Coward, 1982. ISBN: 0-698-30697-X

This should be an easy case for Nate, the greatest of all detectives. All he needs to do is find the lost present Rosamond got him for his birthday. She lost it in the snow, however, there's another problem. She refuses to tell Nate what the present is or even how big it is. This complicates the case, but Nate can overcome any obstacle. This is one in a series of books about the exploits of Nate.

Genre: Mystery
Subject: Finding things
Award: Garden State Children's Book Award, 1985

SHULEVITZ, Uri. *Dawn.* Illus. by the author. Farrar, 1974. ISBN: 0-374-31707-0

The old man and his grandson sleep in darkness on the shore of a lake. The darkness gives way as dawn breaks and the two awaken, moving onto the lake in a boat. As the sun rises, colors come crashing into day in this beautifully illustrated book. Its pictures begin in darkness, brighten with the dawn, and end in a blaze of colors just like the day.

Genre: Realistic fiction
Subjects: Grandparents; nature
Awards: Christopher Award, 1974; Honor List of International Board on Books for Young People, 1976

SLOBODKINA, Esphyr. *Caps for Sale.* Illus. by the author. Young Scott Books, 1947. ISBN: 0-201-09147-X
A peddler has had an unlucky day—he hasn't sold a single cap. He decides to take a walk in the country and then takes a nap under a tree. When he wakes up, his caps are missing. The peddler hunts for them frantically and only when he looks up does he find a group of monkeys wearing the caps. How will the peddler get them back?

Genre: Humor
Subjects: Monkeys; peddlers and peddling

VAN WOERKOM, Dorothy. *Donkey Ysabel.* Illus. by Normand Chartier. Macmillan, 1978. ISBN: 0-02-791280-9
There's been a change on this farm. Nobody needs Ysabel the donkey now that there is a car. That is, no one needs the donkey until there is car trouble. Then everyone wants her—Papa, Mama, Pedro the pig, Carla the goat, and even Pepi the rooster. In the end it is Ysabel to the rescue.

Genre: Humor
Subject: Donkeys

VIORST, Judith. *The Tenth Good Thing about Barney.* Illus. by Erik Blegvad. Atheneum, 1971. ISBN: 0-689-20688-7
Barney, the pet cat, has died, and the boy is sad. The boy's mother thinks he should say ten good things about Barney, but he can only think of nine. One day while working with his father in the garden, the boy thinks of the tenth good thing: Now that Barney's under the ground he's helping plants grow.

Genre: Realistic fiction
Subjects: Death; cats

WABER, Bernard. *An Anteater Named Arthur.* Illus. by the author. Houghton Mifflin, 1967. ISBN: 0-395-20336-8
Arthur doesn't like being an anteater. He especially doesn't like being *called* an anteater. Actually, Arthur doesn't like being an anteater who sometimes has nothing to do, sometimes is too choosy, and sometimes forgets. In this funny story, Arthur's mother tells how he is so upset he won't even eat the red ants for breakfast, wishing for brown ones instead. It seems that Arthur's one pleasure is the warm friendship of his brother.

Genre: Humor
Subjects: Anteaters; family life

WELLS, Rosemary. *Benjamin & Tulip.* Illus. by the author. Dial, 1973. ISBN: 0-8037-2057-2
Benjamin and Tulip are two raccoons who are having a difference of opinion. Tulip wants to fight, and Benjamin doesn't. The squabble leads to an accident that won't make Tulip any happier, although it will certainly stop the argument.

Genre: Realistic fiction
Subject: Raccoons
Award: ALA Notable Children's Books, 1973

WELLS, Rosemary. *Max's New Suit.* Illus. by the author. Dial, 1979. ISBN: 0-8037-6065-5
In this story about a rabbit family, Max hates his sister always telling him how to dress. So one day, he dresses himself, putting his shirt on one *leg* at a time and then the rest of his clothes, for the party he will attend. When Max is through dressing, the new outfit his sister bought him certainly looks odd. This is one in a series of books about Max the rabbit and his older sister Ruby.

Genre: Humor
Subjects: Rabbits; brothers and sisters; clothing and dress

WILLIAMS, Barbara. *Albert's Toothache.* Illus. by Kay Chorao. Dutton, 1974. ISBN: 0-525-25368-8
Everyone knows turtles don't have teeth. So no wonder no one believes that Albert has a toothache. However, Albert's grand-

mother finds the problem and fixes it. Soft brown sketches give the reader a feeling of sympathy for Albert.

Genre: Humor
Subjects: Turtles; teeth; family life

WISEMAN, Bernard. *Morris and Boris.*   Illus. by the author. Dodd, Mead, 1974. ISBN: 0-396-06991-6
Can a moose say "Peter Piper picked a peck of pickled peppers"? Boris the bear wants Morris the moose to learn about riddles, tongue twisters, and playing hide and seek. But Morris just wants to ask questions. No wonder Boris is angry. This is one in a series of books about the unlikely friendship of Morris and Boris.

Genre: Humor
Subjects: Moose; bears

ZION, Gene. *Harry the Dirty Dog.*   Illus. by Margaret Bloy Graham. Harper & Row, 1956 (reissued in 1976). ISBN: 0-06-026865-4
Whoever saw a dog that liked a bath? Harry the dog certainly didn't. He hated baths and avoided them every time he could. However, while wandering through the city after escaping from a bath, he becomes even grimier. Finally, Harry is so dirty that his own family can't recognize him. Now, when he needs attention but no one gives it to him, Harry sees the value of keeping clean. This is one in a series of books about Harry.

Genre: Humor
Subject: Dogs

ZOLOTOW, Charlotte. *Mr. Rabbit and the Lovely Present.* Illus. by Maurice Sendak. Harper & Row, 1962. ISBN: 0-06-026945-6
A little girl wants to give her mother a gift and wonders what would make a good present. She tells Mr. Rabbit that her mother likes red, yellow, green, and blue, so he suggests a yellow taxicab, a green emerald, and a blue lake. But none of these ideas will do. Finally, Mr. Rabbit comes up with just the right present.

Genre: Fantasy
Subjects: Rabbits; color; birthdays
Award: Caldecott Medal Honor Books, 1963

5

Books for the Second Half of Grade Two

Readability: 2.5–2.9

Readers at this age are branching out. While many of the books they choose are still essentially about their own daily lives, there is a sprinkling of folktale and history in the selections in this list.

EASY

Aruego, Jose and Ariane Aruego. *A Crocodile's Tale*
Bemelmans, Ludwig. *Madeleine's Rescue*
Coerr, Eleanor. *The Mixed-Up Mystery Smell*
Daly, Niki. *Joseph's Other Red Sock*
Graham, Margaret Bloy. *Be Nice to Spiders*
———. *Benjy and the Barking Bird*
Greenfield, Eloise. *Me and Neesie*
Hughes, Shirley. *Alfie Gets in First*
———. *Alfie Gives a Hand*
———. *Alfie's Feet*
———. *An Evening at Alfie's*
Lionni, Leo. *Inch by Inch*
Oram, Hiawyn. *In the Attic*
Rayner, Mary. *Mr. and Mrs. Pig's Evening Out*
Schatell, Brian. *Farmer Goff and His Turkey, Sam*
Schwartz, Amy. *Bea and Mr. Jones*
Sharmat, Marjorie Weinman. *Gila Monsters Meet You at the Airport*
Steig, William. *Sylvester and the Magic Pebble*
Udry, Janice M. *What Mary Jo Shared*

EASY (cont.)
Williams, Linda. *The Little Old Lady Who Was Not Afraid of Anything*

AVERAGE
Allen, Linda. *Mr. Simkins' Grandma*
Browne, Anthony. *Gorilla*
Cole, Joanna. *Bony-Legs*
Duvoisin, Roger. *Jasmine*
Emberley, Barbara. *Drummer Hoff*
Gág, Wanda. *Millions of Cats*
———. *Nothing at All*
Gay, Michael. *The Christmas Wolf*
Hoban, Russell. *Bedtime for Frances*
Kellogg, Steven. *The Mysterious Tadpole*
———. *A Rose for Pinkerton*
Levitin, Sonia. *Nobody Stole the Pie*
Lobel, Arnold. *Frog and Toad Together*
Marshall, James. *George and Martha, Rise and Shine*
———. *George and Martha, Tons of Fun*
Nixon, Joan Lowery. *If You Say So, Claude*
Peet, Bill. *Huge Harold*
Pellowski, Michael J. *Benny's Bad Day*
Porte, Barbara Ann. *Harry's Dog*
Selsam, Millicent E. *Night Animals*
Seuling, Barbara. *The Teeny Tiny Woman: An Old English Ghost Tale*
Stevenson, James. *Could Be Worse*
Waber, Bernard. *The House on East 88th Street*
Williams, Vera B. *A Chair for My Mother*
———. *Music, Music for Everyone*
———. *Something Special for Me*
Wood, Audrey. *King Bidgood's in the Bathtub*
Yashima, Taro. *Crow Boy*
Zelinsky, Paul O. *The Maid and the Mouse and the Odd-Shaped House*

CHALLENGING
Aardema, Verna. *The Vingananee and the Tree Toad*
Branley, Franklyn. *Comets*
Coombs, Patricia. *Mouse Cafe*

Domanska, Janina. *The Best of the Bargain*
Guthrie, Donna. *The Witch Who Lives Down the Hall*
Hurd, Edith Thacher. *Mama Don't Allow*
Hutchins, Pat. *The Tale of Thomas Mead*
Keats, Ezra Jack. *Goggles*
Lobel, Arnold. *Grasshopper on the Road*
Schwartz, David M. *How Much Is a Million?*
Stevenson, James. *We Can't Sleep*
Zion, Gene. *The Sugar Mouse Cake*

AARDEMA, Verna. *The Vingananee and the Tree Toad.* Illus. by Ellen Weiss. Warne, 1983. ISBN: 0-7232-6217-9
A vingananee is a big monster that's stronger than a lion and it likes to eat stew. Every time the residents of the house plan stew for dinner, the monster beats up the cook and steals the food. It beats up the rat, the buck, and then the lion. Now it's up to the little tree toad to stop the huge monster, and with the help of a miracle, it does.
Genre: Folklore and fairy tales
Subjects: Animals; folklore (Liberia)

ALLEN, Linda. *Mr. Simkins' Grandma.* Illus. by Loretta Lustig. Morrow, 1979. ISBN: 0-688-22191-2 (o.p.)
One day, an old lady comes to Mr. Simkins's house. She says she is his grandma. Mr. Simkins didn't even know he had a grandmother. It's hard to believe that this lady who acts so strangely really is his grandma. But if she isn't, then who could she be?
Genre: Realistic fiction
Subject: Family life

ARUEGO, Jose and Ariane Aruego. *A Crocodile's Tale.* Illus. by the authors. Scribner, 1972. ISBN: 0-684-12806-3
A crocodile was caught in a trap, and Juan helped it escape. Now the crocodile wants to eat the boy, and there is no one to help him escape. A hat and coat pass by, but pay no heed to the boy's distress because they have been treated unkindly by humans. A monkey, though, has a way to rescue Juan. Along with the excitement of the boy's predicament, the story impresses readers with the value in being thankful.
Genre: Folklore and fairy tales
Subjects: Crocodiles; folklore (Philippines)

BEMELMANS, Ludwig. *Madeleine's Rescue.*   Illus. by the author. Viking, 1953. ISBN: 0-670-44716-1
This is a story of a very smart dog named Genevieve. The dog saves Madeleine from the river and becomes her pet. But this creates a problem. Madeleine's boarding school doesn't allow pets, so what will happen to Genevieve? This is one in a series of books about Madeleine.

Genre: Realistic fiction
Subjects: Dogs; Paris (France); schools; stories in rhyme
Awards: *New York Times* Choice of Best Illustrated Children's Books of the Year, 1953; Caldecott Medal Honor Books, 1954

BRANLEY, Franklyn. *Comets.*   Illus. by Giulio Maestro. Crowell, 1984. ISBN: 0-690-04414-3
Along with pictures and diagrams, this book describes a comet. The explanation covers how comets develop and what they're made of. It discusses Halley's comet and answers such basic questions as why a comet has a tail and where comets travel.

Genre: Nonfiction
Subjects: Comets; Halley's comet

BROWNE, Anthony. *Gorilla.*   Illus. by the author. Knopf, 1985. ISBN: 0-394-87525-7
Hannah is a lonely girl whose best friend is a toy gorilla. Too busy to spend much time with her, Hannah's father has given her the gorilla. Now the girl has to figure out where to take her new friend so that the two of them can have a good time. She comes up with an answer that takes them on a fantastic trip.

Genre: Fantasy
Subjects: Gorillas; fathers and daughters
Awards: Kate Greenaway Medal, 1983; *New York Times* Best Illustrated Children's Books of the Year, 1985

COERR, Eleanor. *The Mixed-Up Mystery Smell.*   Illus. by Tomie dePaola. Putnam, 1976. ISBN: 0-399-20467-9 (o.p.)
When she passed by the old "haunted" house, Kate smelled a strange odor. She caught it in a box for her detective friends to test, but they lost the odor when the box was opened. So the friends decide to visit the "haunted" house to find out what the smell was. What they discover is not frightening at all. Instead,

there is an unexpected surprise, and a recipe is at the end that tells readers how to bake bread.

Genre: Mystery
Subject: Smell

COLE, Joanna. *Bony-Legs.* Illus. by Dirk Zimmer. Four Winds, 1983. ISBN: 0-02-722970-X
The villain of this Russian tale is a terrible witch with iron teeth. Her house is built on chicken feet. When Sasha comes near, the witch captures her. But Sasha has befriended the mean witch's dog and cat, and the three of them find a way to escape.

Genre: Folklore and fairy tales
Subjects: Witches; Baba Yaga (legendary character); folklore (Soviet Union)

COOMBS, Patricia. *Mouse Cafe.* Illus. by the author. Lothrop, 1972. ISBN: 0-688-51379-4 (o.p.)
Two ugly, mean mice make their little sister do all the work. When she gets too tired, the others throw her out of the house. This turns out to be a blessing in disguise for the little mouse. She finds that others in the world are nice and ends up happier than her mean sisters.

Genre: Fantasy
Subject: Mice

DALY, Niki. *Joseph's Other Red Sock.* Illus. by the author. Atheneum, 1982. ISBN: 0-689-50216-8
Joseph has lost a red sock. He imagines a monster in the cupboard has it, and it's the monster that Joseph sees right now. Pulling the monster out of the cupboard and chasing it back in again, Joseph finds his other red sock. But now he only has one blue shoe.

Genre: Humor
Subject: Monsters

DOMANSKA, Janina. *The Best of the Bargain.* Illus. by the author. Greenwillow, 1977. ISBN: 0-688-80062-9
Olek the fox is not very smart. First, Hugo the hedgehog tricks him into giving up all his potatoes. Next, Hugo cheats him out of all his wheat. That's in addition to half his apples both times.

Will Olek ever learn to make a good bargain? Or perhaps it's better not to bargain at all with someone as unfair as Hugo. Bright block colors are used to illustrate Olek and Hugo.

Genre: Folklore and fairy tales
Subjects: Animals; folklore (Poland)

DUVOISIN, Roger. *Jasmine.*   Illus. by the author. Knopf, 1973. ISBN: 0-394-82444-X (o.p.)
The hat that Jasmine the cow found has really caused trouble. She looks so different that all the other barnyard animals want hats, too. They want Jasmine to look like them, but she likes looking different. Her changes really start turmoil in this barnyard.

Genre: Realistic fiction
Subjects: Cows; animals; hats

EMBERLEY, Barbara. *Drummer Hoff.*   Illus. by Ed Emberley. Prentice-Hall, 1967. ISBN: 0-13-220822-9
There was General Border, Major Scott, Captain Bammer, Sergeant Chowder, Corporal Farrell, and Private Parriage. In rhyming narrative each soldier contributes to the assembly and loading of the cannon. Brightly colored woodcuts illustrate the military folk rhyme that ends when Drummer Hoff lights the gun's fire.

Genre: Folklore and fairy tales
Subject: Soldiers
Award: Caldecott Medal Honor Books, 1968

GÁG, Wanda. *Millions of Cats.*   Illus. by the author. Coward, 1977. ISBN: 0-698-20091-8
An old man sets out to find a cat for his wife. He sees millions of cats on a hill but can't decide which to take home. To solve his problem, he takes them all, knowing that he can't keep them. From these millions of cats, he and his wife manage to find just the right cat for their pet. The black-and-white drawings are so full of detail that young readers enjoy studying the pictures over and over again.

Genre: Humor
Subjects: Cats; pets
Award: Newbery Medal Honor Books, 1929

GÁG, Wanda. *Nothing at All.* Illus. by the author. Coward, 1941. ISBN: 0-698-30264-8

Three puppies live in homes near each other and hope to be adopted by kind masters. But one of them has a problem—it is invisible. There's nothing at all there when visitors come. Pointy and Curly, the two visible dogs, are taken away to good homes. But Nothing-at-All is left behind until it finds a way to make itself visible.

Genre: Humor
Subjects: Dogs; pets
Award: Caldecott Medal Honor Books, 1942

GAY, Michael. *The Christmas Wolf.* Illus. by the author. Greenwillow, 1983. ISBN: 0-688-02290-1

When Father Wolf sets out to find Christmas presents for his family, he has no money. He disguises himself and goes shopping but returns from the department store without a present. His luck begins to change when he is hit by a truck. He isn't badly injured and is rescued by Mother Wolf, but the truck drivers are so shaken that they abandon the truck. The good fortune that follows brings presents to everyone after all.

Genre: Adventure
Subjects: Holidays (Christmas); wolves

GRAHAM, Margaret Bloy. *Be Nice to Spiders.* Illus. by the author. Harper & Row, 1967. ISBN: 0-06-022073-2

A little spider enters a cage in the zoo and begins to spin a web. Soon, all the animals and the zookeeper like the spider. In fact, the zookeeper says to be nice to the spider because of what he's doing to help the animals in the zoo.

Genre: Realistic fiction
Subjects: Spiders; animals; zoos

GRAHAM, Margaret Bloy. *Benjy and the Barking Bird.* Illus. by the author. Harper & Row, 1971. ISBN: 0-06-022079-1

Benjy, the dog with the big floppy ears, is the only pet of the family. Everyone loves him, and Benjy loves the members of the family, but Aunt Tilly disturbs the household when she and her pet parrot, Tilly, come to visit. The parrot can bark like a dog and is soon the favorite of the family. Its barking really bothers

Benjy, however, and in desperation the dog throws the bird and its cage into the trash. The cage breaks open and Tilly escapes. In large, clear pictures the book shows the anxiety of family members and the distress of Benjy as they search for Tilly, then finally resort to trickery to get the bird to come back home.

Genre: Adventure
Subjects: Family life; pets (parrots)

GREENFIELD, Eloise. *Me and Neesie.*   Illus. by Moneta Barnett. Crowell, 1975. ISBN: 0-690-00715-9
This is a story about a warm black family with a common problem: An only child with an imaginary friend. Janell's mother doesn't really believe in her daughter's pretend friend, Neesie, but is willing to put up with her, until there is a problem with Aunt Bea. Later when Janell starts school, the need for an imaginary friend vanishes and so does Neesie.

Genre: Realistic fiction
Subject: Imagination

GUTHRIE, Donna. *The Witch Who Lives Down the Hall.*   Illus. by Amy Schwartz. Harcourt, 1985. ISBN: 0-15-298610-3
A boy lives in a big apartment building like all the others in the city, except a witch lives down the hall from him. At least her long hair, blue jogging sneakers, black cat, and the crazy things she does make him think she's a witch. Most of the time, the boy stays away from Mrs. McWee and Malcolm, her cat. But it's fun to be with a witch on Halloween.

Genre: Realistic fiction
Subjects: Holidays (Halloween); witchcraft; neighborliness; apartment houses

HOBAN, Russell. *Bedtime for Frances.*   Illus. by Garth Williams. Harper & Row, 1960. ISBN: 0-06-022350-2
Frances the badger doesn't want to go to bed. She tries all the tricks children use to delay bedtime. But Francis, like most children, has a father who will not be outwitted. This is one of several stories about Frances and her badger family.

Genre: Realistic fiction
Subject: Badgers

HUGHES, Shirley. *Alfie Gets in First.* Illus. by the author. Lothrop, 1982. ISBN: 0-688-00848-8

Alfie goes shopping with his mother. When they get home, Alfie runs ahead and accidentally locks her out of the house. The key and Alfie are on the inside, and Alfie's mother and baby sister, Annie Rose, are on the outside. Alfie can't reach the catch to open the door, so how will Mom and Annie Rose get inside? This is one in a series of books about Alfie and his family.

Genre: Realistic fiction

Subjects: Locks and keys; family life

HUGHES, Shirley. *Alfie Gives a Hand.* Illus. by the author. Lothrop, 1983. ISBN: 0-688-02386-X

Alfie is worried—it's the first time he's been invited to a party. Since his mother and baby sister, Annie Rose, can't come, Alfie decides to take his bit of old blanket. He enjoys the party but won't let go of the blanket. Finally, Alfie must make a brave decision in order to help a friend. This is one in a series of books about Alfie and his family.

Genre: Realistic fiction

Subjects: Parties; blankets; helpfulness

HUGHES, Shirley. *Alfie's Feet.* Illus. by the author. Lothrop, 1982. ISBN: 0-688-01658-8

Alfie gets a shiny new pair of yellow boots. They're the right size, so they should fit. But when Alfie puts them on, they feel funny. Maybe that's because he has mixed up the left and the right boot so that they're on the wrong feet. This is one in a series of books about Alfie and his family.

Genre: Realistic fiction

Subjects: Shoes and boots; left and right

HUGHES, Shirley. *An Evening at Alfie's.* Illus. by the author. Lothrop, 1985. ISBN: 0-688-04122-1

It is a usual evening, when Maureen MacNally, the baby-sitter, comes to watch Alfie and his baby sister, Annie Rose. Annie Rose is asleep in her crib, and Maureen reads Alfie the story of Noah's Ark before putting him to bed. But Alfie doesn't feel sleepy, and before long he hears a strange noise—a pipe has burst and it's raining upstairs. To add to the chaos, Annie Rose wakes up and begins to cry. Now the evening at Alfie's is anything but usual. This is one in a series of books about Alfie and his family.

Genre: Realistic fiction

Subjects: Family life; baby-sitters

HURD, Edith Thacher. *Mama Don't Allow.*   Illus. by the author. Harper & Row, 1984. ISBN: 0-06-022690-0

Miles has a new saxophone, but his mother doesn't want him practicing at home. But Miles and his three-piece Swamp Band must practice because they are going to play for the Alligator Ball. The boys are excited because everyone will come to the dance. However, their excitement is dampened when they find that one item on the menu for the ball is Swamp Band Soup. Miles and his band think quickly and use their musical talents to escape from the hungry alligators.

Genre: Fantasy

Subjects: Boys; music; alligators

HUTCHINS, Pat. *The Tale of Thomas Mead.*   Illus. by the author. Greenwillow, 1980. ISBN: 0-688-80282-6

"Why should I?" says Thomas Mead when people want him to read. So he goes through life as an illiterate. His stubbornness leads to a lot of accidents and a time in jail. Finally, Thomas is convinced by his parents and a policeman that it's time he learned to read.

Genre: Humor

Subjects: Reading; stories in rhyme

KEATS, Ezra Jack. *Goggles.*   Illus. by the author. Macmillan, 1969. ISBN: 0-02-749590-6

Peter finds some goggles and then meets some bullies who are much bigger than he is. The bullies want the goggles. At first, there doesn't seem to be much the boy can do, but then Willie, his dog, has an idea. This is one in a series of books about Peter.

Genre: Realistic fiction

Subjects: Eyeglasses; bullies

Award: Caldecott Medal Honor Books, 1970

KELLOGG, Steven. *The Mysterious Tadpole.*   Illus. by the author. Dial, 1977. ISBN: 0-8037-6245-3
Uncle McAllister has sent Louis a package from a distant country. In the package is a tadpole that Louis names Alphonse. Alphonse turns out to be an unusual tadpole. Where do you keep a tadpole when it gets too big even for a bathtub? Alphonse seems to be growing as large as a monster. Louis's teacher thinks it might be the Loch Ness monster. Finding a place for Alphonse to live takes a whole year, until another gift arrives from Uncle McAllister.

Genre: Humor
Subject: Pets

KELLOGG, Steven. *A Rose for Pinkerton.*   Illus. by the author. Dial, 1981. ISBN: 0-8037-7502-4
Pinkerton the Great Dane and Rose the kitten are an odd pair of companions. Pinkerton's owners have decided the dog needs a friend, but is a kitten really suitable? This dog and cat become such friends that the dog seems to act like a cat and the cat like a dog. Together they have many misadventures until the two find their real identities and return to being just good friends. This is one in a series of books about Pinkerton.

Genre: Humor
Subjects: Dogs; cats
Award: American Institute of Graphic Arts Books Show, 1982

LEVITIN, Sonia. *Nobody Stole the Pie.*   Illus. by Fernando Krahn. Harcourt, 1980. ISBN: 0-15-257469-7
It was the largest pie made from the finest lollyberries. Such a huge pie could feed everyone at the festival in this small town. But when the townspeople were ready to eat, only one piece of pie was left. No one would admit to stealing the rest, but the mayor knew who had stolen the pie.

Genre: Humor
Subject: Pies

LIONNI, Leo. *Inch by Inch.*   Illus. by the author. Astor-Honor, 1962. ISBN: 0-8392-3010-9
The inchworm knows how to measure a flamingo's neck, a robin's tail, and a toucan's beak. But even it can't measure a nightin-

gale's song. The reader will discover that some things in the inchworm's natural world are just immeasurable.

Genre: Concept book
Subjects: Measurement; birds; worms
Awards: *New York Times* Choice of Best Illustrated Children's Books, 1960; Caldecott Medal Honor Books, 1961

LOBEL, Arnold. *Frog and Toad Together.*   Illus. by the author. Harper & Row, 1972. ISBN: 0-06-023959-X
Five short stories tell of the adventures of two friends, Frog and Toad. Frog can't help Toad when he loses his list of things to do. Toad tries to make seeds grow by reciting poetry. Frog and Toad try to exercise their willpower when it comes to eating cookies. Together they practice being brave. Then, when Toad has a dream, Frog appears in it. This is one in a series of books about Frog and Toad. The series was awarded Recognition of Merit by the George G. Stone Center for Children's Books (Claremont, California), 1978.

Genre: Humor
Subjects: Frogs; toads; friendship
Awards: ALA Notable Children's Books, 1972; Newbery Medal Honor Books, 1973

LOBEL, Arnold. *Grasshopper on the Road.*   Illus. by the author. Harper & Row, 1978. ISBN: 0-06-023961-1
In these six short stories, Grasshopper encounters strangers, a worm and a housefly, as he walks along a road. A mosquito in a boat takes him across a puddle, but who is taking whom? Then there are butterflies and dragonflies that busy themselves in the same way everyday. Most of the animals on the road are creatures of habit, but not Grasshopper. He is the one character who welcomes change.

Genre: Realistic fiction
Subjects: Animals; locusts
Award: Garden State Children's Book Award, 1981

MARSHALL, James. *George and Martha, Rise and Shine.*   Illus. by the author. Houghton Mifflin, 1976. ISBN: 0-395-24738-1
George and Martha, two hippo friends, entertain readers in five short stories about their experiences with bragging, itchy in-

sects, picnics, scary movies, and Martha's fan club. This is one in a series of books about George and Martha.

Genre: Humor
Subjects: Friendship; hippopotamuses

MARSHALL, James. *George and Martha, Tons of Fun.*   Illus. by the author. Houghton Mifflin, 1980. ISBN: 0-395-29524-6
The five short stories in this book tell about the friendship between George and Martha, two hippos. The first story is about Martha's feelings being hurt. Then Martha looks for a way to help George control his sweet tooth. In another story Martha's picture is taken and George tries to hypnotize her. Then Martha loses George's birthday gift and must quickly find another. Each story tells of overzealous friendship. This is one in a series of books about the exploits of George and Martha.

Genre: Humor
Subjects: Friendship; hippopotamuses

NIXON, Joan Lowery. *If You Say So, Claude.*   Illus. by Lorinda Bryan Cauley. Warne, 1980. ISBN: 0-7232-6183-0
Claude, the little man with the big, gray whiskers, and Shirley, his tall, thin wife, leave noisy Colorado Territory to find peace and quiet in the frontier land of Texas. Shirley dislikes Texas with its rattlesnakes, wolves, and wild hogs. But in the end it is Claude who needs to be convinced that Texas is a good place to stay. Framed, brilliantly colored, slightly exaggerated paintings show Claude and Shirley encountering one obstacle after another in their search for a quiet place to live.

Genre: Humor
Subjects: Frontier and pioneer life; Texas; history

ORAM, Hiawyn. *In the Attic.*   Illus. by Satoshi Kitamura. Holt, 1985. ISBN: 0-03-002462-5
The boy in this story has nothing to do, so he takes a trip up into the dark attic. There he can have adventures with any animal he can imagine. Among his friends in the attic are playful mice and a very large tiger.

Genre: Fantasy
Subject: Imagination

PEET, Bill. *Huge Harold.*   Illus. by the author. Houghton Mifflin, 1961. ISBN: 0-395-18449-5
Harold is one strange rabbit — he's as huge as a horse. Frightened by a rabbit so large, some hunters are after him. Harold lives through months of running before he meets Orville B. Croft, who stops the chase and brings the story to a happy but surprising end.

Genre: Humor
Subjects: Rabbits; stories in rhyme

PELLOWSKI, Michael J. *Benny's Bad Day.* Illus. by Doug Cushman. Troll, 1986. ISBN: 0-8167-0620-4
Everything Benny the bear does all day turns out to be a mess. He makes himself a jelly sandwich for lunch and in the process spills the jelly everywhere. Then, when he starts to eat the sandwich, it ends up all over his shirt. And that is just the start of what happens on a very bad day for Benny.

Genre: Realistic fiction
Subject: Luck

PORTE, Barbara Ann. *Harry's Dog.* Illus. by Yossi Abolafia. Greenwillow, 1984. ISBN: 0-688-02555-2
After Harry gets a pet dog, he finds that his father is allergic to her. Harry tries everything, but there is no way he can keep the dog. Everyone feels terrible until Aunt Rose thinks of a solution.

Genre: Realistic fiction
Subject: Pets

RAYNER, Mary. *Mr. and Mrs. Pig's Evening Out.*   Illus. by the author. Atheneum, 1976. ISBN: 0-689-30530-3
Mr. and Mrs. Pig seem to find a nice baby-sitter, Mrs. Wolf, for their ten little pigs. Who would suspect she wants pig for dinner? The suspense builds as Mrs. Wolf carries off one of the brothers to a warm oven in the kitchen. Her plans go awry, though, when the other piglets find a way to beat her at her own game.

Genre: Humor
Subjects: Pigs; baby-sitters; cleverness

SCHATELL, Brian. *Farmer Goff and His Turkey, Sam.*   Illus. by the author. Lippincott, 1982. ISBN: 0-397-31982-7

Farmer Goff has a turkey named Sam that has won prizes at fairs, which has saved Sam from becoming Farmer Goff's dinner. Sam loves pies, and the farmer enters him in a fair, which also has a pie-baking contest. While being judged, Sam spots Mrs. Goff's pies and eats all 294 of them. The farmer is disgruntled, and is likely to have Sam for dinner. This is the first in a series about Farmer Goff and his turkey, Sam.

Genre: Humor
Subjects: Turkeys; farmers; fairs

SCHWARTZ, Amy. *Bea and Mr. Jones.* Illus. by the author. Bradbury, 1982. ISBN: 0-02-781430-0
Bea is tired of kindergarten, and Mr. Jones is tired of work. So they decide to trade jobs. Surprisingly, the trade is a good one. Mr. Jones is a great helper to the kindergarten teacher and Bea becomes a corporate executive in this unusual turn of events.

Genre: Humor
Subjects: Fathers; school stories; work

SCHWARTZ, David M. *How Much Is a Million?* Illus. by Steven Kellogg. Lothrop, 1985. ISBN: 0-688-04049-7
Not long ago a million was a number too large to even think about. But now we travel millions of miles into space and spend billions of dollars in government. This book illustrates in words and pictures just what these large numbers mean. A person could count to a million in about 22 days at the rate of one count a second. A billion goldfish would fill a football stadium, and the examples continue. Through these examples large numbers are given a meaning readers can picture and understand.

Genre: Nonfiction
Subjects: Number concepts (million, billion, trillion)

SELSAM, Millicent E. *Night Animals.* Illus. with photographs. Four Winds, 1979. ISBN: 0-590-07755-4
Many beautiful and strange animals move around when it is dark. Through photographs and straightforward text, readers come to know such animals as screeching owls, bullfrogs, deer, flying squirrels, moths, opossums, beavers, bats, and weasels.

Genre: Nonfiction
Subject: Nocturnal animals

SEULING, Barbara. *The Teeny Tiny Woman: An Old English Ghost Tale.* Illus. by the author. Penguin, 1978. ISBN: 0-14-050266-1

A very tiny woman goes out one night to a graveyard. She finds a very small bone on top of a grave and takes it home, where she stores it in a cupboard. A teeny tiny voice from the cupboard asks her to give the bone back, then gets a teeny tiny bit louder. As the ghost tale progresses, the loudness increases until the teeny tiny woman in her teeny tiny voice ends the tale with an answer.

Genre: Folklore and fairy tales
Subjects: Ghosts; folklore (England)

SHARMAT, Marjorie Weinman. *Gila Monsters Meet You at the Airport.* Illus. by Byron Barton. Macmillan, 1980. ISBN: 0-02-782450-0

The boy in this story is worried because his family will be moving from New York to a new house out West, a wild place with cactus and buffalo. The rumor is that Gila monsters are there to meet you at the airport. Instead, the boy meets someone his own age who is moving East and is full of his own worries about gangsters and the rumor that airplanes fly through your bedroom window. Reality and fantasy are distinguished in the boys' all-too-real predicament, as their imaginary ideas are set in cloudlike frames.

Genre: Realistic fiction
Subjects: Moving; the West (U.S.); perception

STEIG, William. *Sylvester and the Magic Pebble.* Illus. by the author. Windmill, 1969. ISBN: 0-671-96022-9

Sylvester the donkey collects pebbles, and this time he's found one that's magical. When he holds the rock and makes a wish, the wish comes true. Sylvester wishes he were a rock to save himself from a lion, but then can't hold the magic pebble to change back again. No one looking for Sylvester will recognize him unless the rock is somehow transformed.

Genre: Fantasy
Subjects: Donkeys; magic
Awards: Caldecott Medal Honor Books, 1970; Finalist National Book Awards, 1970

STEVENSON, James. *Could Be Worse.*   Illus. by the author. Greenwillow, 1977. ISBN: 0-688-80075-0

When Mary Ann and Louie tell Grandpa their troubles, he always says the same thing: "It could be worse." Then one day he tells them an exciting story about himself. Full of peril and danger, his adventures take him over land, under sea, and through the air. At the story's end he asks his grandchildren what they think of all this misfortune, and readers can easily predict what the children say. This is one in a series of books with imaginative stories about Grandpa, Mary Ann, and Louie.

Genre: Fantasy

Subjects: Grandfathers; dreams

STEVENSON, James. *We Can't Sleep.*   Illus. by the author. Greenwillow, 1982. ISBN: 0-688-01213-2

Mary Ann and Louie can't sleep, so Grandpa tells them a story. It all starts when he runs 20 miles and hitches a ride on the fin of a shark. Then he jumps over an iceberg and encounters polar bears, walruses, a fire-breathing dragon, and a hurricane. Meanwhile, the children grow so tired that it's easy to predict what will happen by the time Grandpa's story ends. This is one in a series of books with imaginative stories about Grandpa, Mary Ann, and Louie.

Genre: Fantasy

Subjects: Grandfathers; sleep

Award: Christopher Awards, 1982

UDRY, Janice M. *What Mary Jo Shared.*   Illus. by Eleanor Mill. Whitman, 1966. ISBN: 0-8075-8842-3

Mary Jo had a real problem. She needed to share something in school, but everything she thought of had already been shared by one of her friends. Mary Jo is telling her father about the problem when suddenly she has an idea. The next day she has something very unusual to share with the class, and her father, a doctor, goes along to help. This is one in a series of books about Mary Jo.

Genre: Realistic fiction

Subjects: School stories; families

WABER, Bernard. *The House on East 88th Street.* Illus. by the author. Houghton Mifflin, 1962. ISBN: 0-395-18157-7
Mr. and Mrs. Primm and their son Joshua have just moved into an apartment on 88th Street. Joshua notices something strange in the bathtub—a crocodile the family names Lyle. In spite of everyone's worries about Lyle, he soon proves to be a great asset to the Primm family and to Signor Valenti, a neighbor. This is one in a series of books about Lyle the crocodile.

Genre: Fantasy
Subjects: Crocodiles; New York City

WILLIAMS, Linda. *The Little Old Lady Who Was Not Afraid of Anything.* Illus. by Megan Lloyd. Crowell, 1986. ISBN: 0-690-04586-7
The little old lady doesn't seem to be afraid as she starts a walk through the forest, but her bravery is really tested as she is confronted by a black cat, a cap, and other Halloweenlike subjects that might frighten anyone. For each encounter, the little old lady finds a way to meet the real and imagined threats. By the end of the story, the little old lady has really proven that she is not afraid of anything.

Genre: Realistic fiction
Subjects: Women; fear

WILLIAMS, Vera B. *A Chair for My Mother.* Illus. by the author. Greenwillow, 1982. ISBN: 0-688-00914-X
The mother in a single-parent household works very hard as a waitress, earning money to care for Rosa and her grandmother. A fire destroys their home and all of their belongings. With the help of friends and neighbors, the family gathers enough household goods to set up house once again. They have some basic furniture, but what they want is a big comfortable armchair for the hardworking mother. So they dream and save until the day they can finally buy one. This is one in a series of books about Rosa and her family.

Genre: Realistic fiction
Subjects: Single-parent family; saving and thrift
Awards: Caldecott Medal Honor Books, 1983; *Boston Globe-Horn* Book Awards (illustration), 1983; Other Award, 1984

WILLIAMS, Vera B. *Music, Music for Everyone.* Illus. by the author. Greenwillow, 1984. ISBN: 0-688-02603-6
Grandmother is sick. Rosa, to cheer her up, plays the accordian. This leads to the beginning of the Oak Street Band, an ensemble created out of the girl's love. Soon Rosa earns money to help meet expenses while her grandmother is ill. The music alone is enough to make anyone feel better. This is one in a series of books about Rosa and her family.

Genre: Realistic fiction
Subjects: Family life; bands (music); grandmothers

WILLIAMS, Vera B. *Something Special for Me.* Illus. by the author. Greenwillow, 1983. ISBN: 0-688-01806-8
Rosa's family saves coins in a large jar. Although the jar is not yet full, her mother thinks it's time for Rosa to spend some of the money on herself for a birthday present. Rosa and her mother go from store to store while Rosa tries to decide what to buy. She has a hard time deciding but finally buys a present the whole family can enjoy. This is one in a series of books about Rosa and her family.

Genre: Realistic fiction
Subjects: Family life; gifts

WOOD, Audrey. *King Bidgood's in the Bathtub.* Illus. by the author. Harcourt, 1985. ISBN 0-15-242730-9
Young King Bidgood is in charge of a beautiful kingdom that needs his attention. But the king has decided to take a bath. The bath is so wonderful that Bidgood decides to stay in the bathtub. No matter how urgent the business of the kingdom gets, King Bidgood refuses to leave his bath.

Genre: Fantasy
Subjects: Kings; royalty; baths

YASHIMA, Taro. *Crow Boy.* Illus. by the author. Viking, 1955. ISBN: 0-670-24931-9
In Japan a new boy appears at the school in town. No one seems to know where the boy is from and the other children don't befriend him. He's different from them, very quiet and alone. Day after day, year after year, the boy comes silently to school. It is not until the last day that the other children discover the special

talent that Chiti the Crow Boy has for imitating the calls of a crow.

Genre: Realistic fiction
Subjects: School stories; Japan; individuality
Awards: Child Study Children's Book Committee at Bank Street College Award, 1955; Caldecott Medal Honor Books, 1956

ZELINSKY, Paul O. *The Maid and the Mouse and the Odd-Shaped House.*   Illus. by the author. Dodd, Mead, 1981. ISBN: 0-396-07938-5
The mouse has moved into a new house and has a maid. It is a strange house that takes an unusual shape as the maid cleans each room. Gradually, the rooms develop into a form, one that inspires the mouse and the maid to run very fast. The house in this fanciful story has turned into a *cat!*

Genre: Fantasy
Subjects: Houses; mice; stories in rhyme

ZION, Gene. *The Sugar Mouse Cake.*   Illus. by Margaret Bloy Graham. Scribner, 1964. ISBN: 0-684-13356-3 (o.s.i.)
Tom was the ninth assistant pastry cook, so no one knew if he could really cook—that is, no one except Tina, the mouse who visited Tom at night. When the king needs a new Chief Pastry Cook, Tom enters the baking contest. He decides to decorate his cake with sugar sculptures of mice, an idea he got from Tina. But in the process, a music box falls into the cake, and just as the judging is about to begin, a sugar mouse is broken. Tina takes that mouse's place, and the cake looks beautiful again. But when Tina twitches, the whole tasting party is upset.

Genre: Humor
Subject: Mice

6

Books for the First Half of Grade Three
Readability: 3.0–3.4

Third graders are capable of handling much more sophisticated stories. This list is limited to books of sophisticated ideas and presentations appealing to today's third grader.

EASY

Bang, Molly. *The Paper Crane*
Cole, Babette. *The Trouble with Mom*
Daugherty, James. *Andy and the Lion*
Duvoisin, Roger. *Petunia, I Love You*
Gage, Wilson. *The Crow and Mrs. Gaddy*
Goffstein, M. B. *Fish for Supper*
Heine, Helme. *The Most Wonderful Egg in the World*
Hoff, Syd. *The Litter Knight*
Ness, Evaline. *Sam, Bangs & Moonshine*
Quackenbush, Robert. *Detective Mole and the Circus Mystery*
Schweninger, Ann. *Birthday Wishes*

AVERAGE

Brown, Marcia. *Once a Mouse; A Fable Cut in Wood*
———. *Stone Soup*
Carrick, Carol. *Dark and Full of Secrets*
dePaola, Tomie. *Strega Nona*
Galdone, Paul. *The Elves and the Shoemaker*
Hancock, Sibyl. *Old Blue*
Haseley, Dennis. *The Old Banjo*
Isadora, Rachel. *Ben's Trumpet*

AVERAGE (cont.)

Lionni, Leo. *Alexander and the Wind-Up Mouse*
Ormondroyd, Edward. *Broderick*
———. *Theodore*
Turkle, Brinton. *Do Not Open*
Waber, Bernard. *Lyle, Lyle, Crocodile*

CHALLENGING

Brenner, Barbara. *Wagon Wheels*
Clifton, Lucille. *Everett Anderson's Goodbye*
Lewis, Thomas P. *Hill of Fire*
Lionni, Leo. *Frederick*
Mathis, Sharon Bell. *The Hundred Penny Box*
Segal, Lore. *The Story of Mrs. Lovewright and Purrless the Cat*
Turkle, Brinton. *Obadiah the Bold*
Yolen, Jane. *Sleeping Ugly*

BANG, Molly. *The Paper Crane.* Illus. by the author. Greenwillow, 1985. ISBN: 0-688-04108-6

There had not been many guests in the once busy restaurant since it was bypassed by a new highway. One evening, an old man comes in for a meal. He has no money to pay for it, but the owner feeds him anyway. In return, the old man gives the owner a paper crane, which brings him good fortune. Although made of paper, the magical crane can fly, and this draws customers into the restaurant until the old man returns to take the paper crane away. The detailed, full-page illustrations, along with the story of kindness and reward, appeal to readers of all ages.

Genre: Fantasy
Subjects: Magic; birds (cranes); folklore

BRENNER, Barbara. *Wagon Wheels.* Illus. by Don Bolognese. Harper & Row, 1978. ISBN: 0-06-020668-3

Three boys, Willie, Johnny, and Little Brother, and their widowed father decide to move west to improve their fortunes. They find a place near other farms and dig a room to live in. But the land is poor and farming is difficult. After much struggle, the father leaves the oldest boy in charge and travels farther west to seek a better place. When winter arrives, the boys are near starvation. With the help of some neighbors and Indians, the boys manage to survive. Then, one day, the boys receive a message to go west. After a trip of 150 unfamiliar miles, the boys are reunited with their father. The story is based on a real experience of a pioneer family in Nebraska.

Genre: Historical fiction
Subjects: Frontier and pioneer life; history

BROWN, Marcia. *Once a Mouse; A Fable Cut in Wood.* Illus. by the author. Scribner, 1961. ISBN: 0-684-12662-1
A magician saves a tiny mouse from larger enemies. He changes the mouse into bigger and bigger animals until the tiny animal becomes a fierce and awesome tiger. But now the man is in trouble because he has no magic to make the tiger behave. This book is illustrated with award-winning woodcuts in olives, yellows, and reds.

Genre: Folklore and fairy tales
Subjects: Animals; folklore (India)
Awards: *New York Times* Choice of Best Illustrated Children's Books of the Year, 1961; Caldecott Medal Honor Books, 1962

BROWN, Marcia. *Stone Soup.* Illus. by the author. Scribner, 1947 (reissued 1975). ISBN: 0-684-92296-7
Three tired and hungry soldiers are returning from battle. They approach a village of people who hide their food and close their doors. No one offers help to the soldiers, but the soldiers have a plan. They build a fire under a large pot of water, then place stones inside. Curious townspeople come to see the preparation of this strange stone soup, which in the end is full of vegetables and meats. The soldiers are highlighted by pen-and-ink drawings, with spots of red to direct the eyes of the young reader.

Genre: Folklore and fairy tales
Subject: Folklore (France)
Award: Caldecott Medal Honor Books, 1948

CARRICK, Carol. *Dark and Full of Secrets.* Illus. by Donald Carrick. Clarion, 1984. ISBN: 0-89919-271-8
Christopher and his father go snorkling so the boy can overcome his fear of what is under a nearby pond. Because Christopher is not a good swimmer, he stays in shallow water. The pond's water is dark and exciting and there are many interesting things to see.

Christopher gets so interested in what he is doing that he forgets to stay close to the shore. As he grows tired, he discovers that he has strayed into deep water and needs to be rescued.

Genre: Adventure
Subjects: Ponds; skin diving

CLIFTON, Lucille. *Everett Anderson's Goodbye.* Illus. by Ann Grifalconi. Holt, 1983. ISBN: 0-03-063518-7
Everett Anderson's father has died. This story reveals Everett's thoughts as he works through denial, anger, bargaining, depression, and acceptance of the death and is finally able to go on with his own life. Detailed black-and-white drawings add to the feeling of anguish as Everett thinks about what it means to die.

Genre: Realistic fiction
Subjects: Death; fathers and sons; stories in rhyme

COLE, Babette. *The Trouble with Mom.* Illus. by the author. Coward, 1984. ISBN: 0-698-20624-X.
The boy in this story has a real problem. His mother is a witch, and even when she is being careful, she manages to stir up trouble. She "drives" to school on a broomstick — and that is only one of her differences. His mother becomes unpopular, but then the school catches on fire and she uses her witchcraft to save the day.

Genre: Fantasy
Subject: Witches

DAUGHERTY, James. *Andy and the Lion.* Illus. by the author. Viking, 1938 (reissued 1966). ISBN: 0-670-12433-8
Andy wanted a book about lions. He found one in the library that took him on such imaginary adventures that he soon began to dream about lions. Thinking about lions was fun until one day he saw a "lion" on the way to school. Fearful at first, Andy and the lion eventually become fast friends. The story is told in few words and is illustrated with black and gold pictures filled with action that captures the reader's attention.

Genre: Adventure
Subjects: Lions; friendship
Award: Caldecott Medal Honor Books, 1939

dePAOLA, Tomie. *Strega Nona.* Illus. by the author. Prentice-Hall, 1975. ISBN: 0-13-851600-6
Strega Nona is a witch who has a magic pot that cooks pasta for her whenever she wants it to. One day Strega Nona goes off and leaves the pot with Big Anthony, giving him strict instructions not to use it. Naturally, Big Anthony has to try the pot. It works; the pot produces delicious pasta but there is a small problem. He has not learned how to stop the pot. By the time Strega Nona returns, there is pasta everywhere. And there is no way to clean it up except for Big Anthony to eat his way out of the mess.

Genre: Folklore and fairy tales
Subjects: Folklore (Italy); witches
Awards: Caldecott Medal Honor Books, 1976; Brooklyn Art Books for Children Citations, 1977

DUVOISIN, Roger. *Petunia, I Love You.* Illus. by the author. Knopf, 1965. ISBN: 0-394-90870-8
A raccoon follows Petunia the goose everywhere. Petunia seems not to know that the raccoon eats other animals and would "love" to eat a nice fat goose such as she. The crafty raccoon follows Petunia until finally it has a good plan for catching her for dinner. In the end, the raccoon is forced to make a sudden change of plans. This is one in a series of stories in which Petunia always seems to come out on top in spite of herself.

Genre: Adventure
Subjects: Geese; raccoons

GAGE, Wilson. *The Crow and Mrs. Gaddy.* Illus. by Marylin Hafner. Greenwillow, 1984. ISBN: 0-688-02535-8
The crow and Mrs. Gaddy are continually playing tricks on each other. First, the crow does something mean and then Mrs. Gaddy follows suit. For example, he eats her corn so she plants pebbles in anticipation of his next visit. It's one dirty trick after another until finally Mrs. Gaddy finds a way to win the crow over.

Genre: Humor
Subject: Crows

GALDONE, Paul. *The Elves and the Shoemaker.* Based on Lucy Crane's translation from the German of the Brothers Grimm. Illus. by the author. Clarion, 1984. ISBN: 0-89919-226-2

In this retelling of the classic tale, a very poor shoemaker cuts his last bit of leather for a pair of shoes that he will sew the next day. But the next morning, the shoemaker finds the shoes have already been sewn. As the days pass, the shoemaker finds more fine shoes newly made every morning. Finally, curiosity makes the shoemaker find a way to discover how the shoes are finished.

Genre: Folklore and fairy tales
Subjects: Folklore (Germany); elves; shoes

GOFFSTEIN, M. B. *Fish for Supper.* Illus. by the author. Dial, 1976. ISBN: 0-8037-2572-8

It's always the same. Every evening Grandma has a fresh fish dinner and goes to bed early. Then she gets up at five in the morning and rushes down to the beach to fish again. She catches all kinds of fish, then brings them home for her evening dinner. Small black-and-white line drawings illustrate Grandma and her love for fishing.

Genre: Realistic fiction
Subjects: Grandmothers; fishing
Award: Caldecott Medal Honor Books, 1977

HANCOCK, Sibyl. *Old Blue.* Illus. by Erick Ingraham. Putnam, 1980. ISBN: 0-399-61141-X

Davy, Cookie, and Pa are driving a herd of longhorn steer on the trail. They find an unexpected helper in Old Blue, a longhorn that becomes a friend of the cowboys. Old Blue takes charge of leading the herd on the trail. Then, when they stop for the night, the animal beds down with the three men, like any other cowhand. Softly muted illustrations in black, white, gray, and blue help establish the feeling of loneliness and friendship on the drive.

Genre: Historical fiction
Subjects: Cattle; cowhands; West (U.S.)

HASELEY, Dennis. *The Old Banjo.* Illus. by Stephen Gammell. Macmillan, 1983. ISBN: 0-02-743100-2

Musical instruments are all over the farm—a banjo, a violin, a trombone, a trumpet. The instruments are just lying around abandoned. They remain idle until one evening the banjo begins to remember the old days and the beautiful music all the instruments made when they played together. What happens next even draws the farmer from his work. Beautiful black-and-white illustrations add detail to the fanciful story.

Genre: Fantasy
Subject: Musical instruments

HEINE, Helme. *The Most Wonderful Egg in the World.* Illus. by the author. Atheneum, 1983. ISBN: 0-689-50280-X
The three hens in this story are proud and vain. They argue about which is the most beautiful and agree to let the king decide. But the king believes that what they do is more important than how they look, and this leads to an egg-laying contest. The hen who lays the most wonderful egg will become a princess. Each of their eggs is exceptional in its own way, so choosing the winner is difficult.

Genre: Fantasy
Subjects: Chickens; eggs; individuality

HOFF, Syd. *The Litter Knight.* Illus. by the author. McGraw-Hill, 1970. ISBN: 0-07-02918-8 (o.p.)
A young man is dressed like a knight and wants to be one, although he has no way to prove how brave he is. This is because he does not like to fight, even against dragons. Finally, the young knight finds a foe to vanquish and in the process becomes a popular figure because he has rid the kingdom of trash.

Genre: Humor
Subjects: Knights; litter

ISADORA, Rachel. *Ben's Trumpet.* Illus. by the author. Greenwillow, 1979. ISBN: 0-688-80194-3
Ben, a young boy, lives in a Harlem tenement. Every night he can hear the music of the band that plays across the street. Pretending he has a trumpet, Ben sits out on the fire escape of his apartment and plays. Others in the neighborhood see him pretending and tease him for having no trumpet. But Ben's interest in the

band leads to getting his own musical instrument and playing real music.

Genre: Realistic fiction
Subjects: Musicians; jazz music; trumpets
Award: Caldecott Medal Honor Books, 1980

LEWIS, Thomas P. *Hill of Fire.* Illus. by Joan Sandin. Harper & Row, 1971. ISBN: 0-06-023803-8
Near a village in Mexico, a farmer was tending his field when he noticed smoke coming from one spot. As he watched, a volcano began to grow and started to pour out ash and lava. The new volcano grew rapidly until the fields were covered and the village had to be abandoned. What happened and how the land was reinhabited form a realistic story of the volcano Paricutin and its effect on people.

Genre: Historical fiction
Subjects: Mexico; Paricutin (Mexico)

LIONNI, Leo. *Alexander and the Wind-Up Mouse.* Illus. by the author. Pantheon, 1969. ISBN: 0-394-90914-3
A small mouse named Alexander has only one friend. He calls his friend Willie, but Willie can't answer him because it's a toy. The toy is so big and beautiful that Alexander would like to be just like it. Willie has a wind-up key and Alexander wants one too but then changes his mind. With the help of a magic lizard, Alexander finds his friend turned into a real live companion. Collage is used to provide rich illustrations that emphasize the magic and the mystery of this friendship.

Genre: Fantasy
Subject: Mice
Awards: Christopher Award, 1969; Caldecott Medal Honor Books, 1970

LIONNI, Leo. *Frederick.* Illus. by the author. Pantheon, 1966. ISBN: 0-394-91040-0
All the mice are busily working to store food and firewood for the winter—that is, all are working except Frederick. He is busy, but not with collecting food and firewood. Winter arrives and the days and nights grow long and monotonous. Now is the time when the other mice learn that Frederick, a poet, has stored one

of the most important things of all. Lionni's award-winning pictures feature well-rounded mice and backgrounds whose colors change with the seasons.

Genre: Fantasy
Subject: Mice
Awards: *New York Times* Choice of Best Illustrated Children's Books of the Year, 1967; Caldecott Medal Honor Books, 1968

MATHIS, Sharon Bell. *The Hundred Penny Box.* Illus. by Leo Dillon and Diane Dillon. Viking, 1975. ISBN: 0-670-38787-8
Michael's mother wants to throw out an old box that belongs to his 100-year-old great-great-aunt. The box doesn't seem to be worth much. It only has 100 pennies in it, but Michael knows that Aunt Dew has saved the pennies as memories of the events in her life. Keeping the box is important to her, and in the end the boy manages to save it and his aunt's memories. The illustrations are framed in the soft brown shape of an old box.

Genre: Realistic fiction
Subjects: Family life; elderly
Award: Newbery Medal Honor Books, 1976

NESS, Evaline. *Sam, Bangs & Moonshine.* Illus. by the author. Holt, 1966. ISBN: 0-03-080111-7
Samantha, who lived with her father in a village by the sea, had a habit of not telling the truth. She told stories about a fierce lion she had at home when her pet was really a gentle cat, Bangs. She said her mother was a mermaid. There were few people who could tell stranger stories than Sam. One day she pretended to have a pet kangaroo and told her friend Thomas that it had just escaped behind the blue rock in a dangerous spot on the coast. Thomas and Bangs go searching for the imaginary kangaroo. Sam didn't know that a storm was coming or that there was danger from the tides. When her father hears her story about her pet, he hurries to rescue Thomas and Bangs. Thomas is rescued, but Bangs is washed away by the great waves. Before Bangs returns, after being cast ashore at the lighthouse, Sam has plenty of time to think about spreading "moonshine."

Genre: Realistic fiction
Subject: Lying
Award: Caldecott Medal Honor Books, 1967

ORMONDROYD, Edward. *Broderick.* Illus. by John Larrecq. Houghton Mifflin, 1969. ISBN: 0-686-86580-4
Broderick the mouse likes to eat books. He lives in Tim's house and comes out at night to nibble on Tim's books. As he nibbles on a cover, Broderick becomes interested in the pictures and begins to read. The book is about famous mice and now Broderick wonders how he can make his mark in the world. Days pass and he turns to a book about surfing. This inspires him to make a surfboard from a tongue depressor and try his skill on the water. With practice, he is ready to make a name for himself as a world-famous surfer.

Genre: Fantasy
Subjects: Mice; surfing

ORMONDROYD, Edward. *Theodore.* Illus. by John Larrecq. Houghton Mifflin, 1984. ISBN: 0-395-36610-0
Lucy has played with her toy bear Theodore until he is very dirty. Lucy likes him that way, but one day Theodore is caught up with the laundry and dumped into a washing machine at the laundromat. On the way home, he accidentally falls from the laundry basket and is lost. Riding her tricycle, Lucy sees Theodore, but he is so clean that she doesn't even recognize him. The bear might have a chance of being found if only he could get dirty again. This is the first in a series of books about Theodore.

Genre: Realistic fiction
Subject: Toys

QUACKENBUSH, Robert. *Detective Mole and the Circus Mystery.* Illus. by the author. Lothrop, 1985. ISBN: 0-688-04640-1
The star of the circus, a tattooed cow, is missing and the great Detective Mole has been called in to investigate. A blackmail artist tries to interfere, but the detective will not waver from the task at hand. He follows the trail of clues to a picture of a butterfly and finally to the missing star, who is just trying to run away from it all. This is one in a series of books about the dauntless detective.

Genre: Mystery
Subject: Moles

SCHWENINGER, Ann. *Birthday Wishes.* Illus. by the author. Viking, 1986. ISBN: 0-670-80740-7

In comic-strip form, the pictures and sing-sentence comments by the characters tell about the preparation for a birthday by Buttercup the rabbit and her family and friends. Her mother shops for party supplies, and all her friends look for just the right presents. On Buttercup's birthday a special cake is made and the house is decorated for the party. The joyous pictures of the rabbit family and friends illustrate the fun of anticipation and everyone's happiness at the birthday party.

Genre: Realistic fiction
Subjects: Family life; birthdays

SEGAL, Lore. *The Story of Mrs. Lovewright and Purrless the Cat.* Illus. by Paul O. Zelinsky. Farrar, 1985. ISBN: 0-394-86817-X
Mrs. Lovewright wanted a kitten to sit in her lap, purr, and keep her company in the lonely evenings in front of the fire. The groceryman brought her a kitten, but the kitten would not purr. In fact, it wouldn't do any of the things Mrs. Lovewright wanted it to do. Purrless the cat would not sit on her lap. Instead, it liked to take up space on her footstool, or slide down her legs with claws spread, or nip at her toes. It even slept right in the middle of Mrs. Lovewright's bed. However, the cat grew and grew. It didn't seem to be the right kind of pet at all. Finally, Mrs. Lovewright decided to get rid of Purrless.

Genre: Humor
Subject: Pets

TURKLE, Brinton. *Do Not Open.* Illus. by the author. Dutton, 1981. ISBN: 0-525-28785-X
The bottle says "Do not open," but Miss Moody disregards the warning and out comes a snarling monster. Someone else might be worried, but Miss Moody is a doer, not a worrier. She and her cat, Captain Kidd, soon find a way to dispose of the monster. The cat is pictured larger than life, adding to the fanciful nature of the story.

Genre: Fantasy
Subjects: Seashore; cats; magic; monsters

TURKLE, Brinton. *Obadiah the Bold.* Illus. by the author. Penguin, 1985. ISBN: 0-14-050233-5

Set in Nantucket about 100 years ago, the story centers on a boy in a Quaker family. Obadiah dreams of going to sea, sometimes imagining himself as a pirate. But his brothers think Obadiah is too timid to be a seaman or a pirate, and he is easy to scare when he plays pirate with them. Obadiah is downhearted until he sees pictures of his grandfather. He looks just like him and learns that his grandfather had been a ship's captain. Suddenly it seems possible for Obadiah's own dreams of the sea to come true. This is one in a series of stories about the young Quaker boy.

Genre: Historical fiction
Subjects: Society of Friends; Nantucket (Mass.)

WABER, Bernard. *Lyle, Lyle, Crocodile.* Illus. by the author. Houghton Mifflin, 1965. ISBN: 0-395-16995-X
Lyle the crocodile is quite content living with the Primm family. He makes himself useful, helping Joshua with his schoolwork and playing with the children in the neighborhood. But the crocodile scares Mr. Gump's cat and is therefore sent to the zoo. Lyle escapes the zoo and returns home to discover a fire at Mr. Gump's house. This is one in a series of books about the friendly crocodile.

Genre: Adventure
Subjects: Crocodiles; New York City; pets
Award: Lewis Carroll Shelf Award, 1979

YOLEN, Jane. *Sleeping Ugly.* Illus. by Diane Stanley. Coward, 1981. ISBN: 0-698-30721-6
Princess Miserella and Plain Jane are opposites. One is beautiful, and the other might even be considered ugly. But the beautiful-looking one is ugly inside and Plain Jane is a beautiful person inside. When the prince comes to choose his bride, a fairy decides to help in the decision. She puts everyone to sleep and changes things so the prince will wake up the one who will make the best wife for himself. In the end, the beauty of Plain Jane is clear to everyone.

Genre: Fantasy
Subject: Beauty (personal)

7

Books for the Second Half of Grade Three
Readability: 3.5–3.9

Students with a reading vocabulary at this level can read most children's books. Choosing then becomes a matter of the book with the most interesting story.

EASY

Gramatky, Hardie. *Little Toot*
Holabird, Katharine. *Angelina and the Princess*
———. *Angelina Ballerina*
Hurd, Edith Thacher. *I Dance in My Red Pajamas*
Raskin, Ellen. *Spectacles*
Ryan, Cheli Durán. *Hildilid's Night*
Sendak, Maurice. *Where the Wild Things Are*

AVERAGE

Cohen, Barbara. *The Carp in the Bathtub*
Goble, Paul. *The Girl Who Loved Wild Horses*
Lasker, Joe. *Nick Joins In*
MacLachlan, Patricia. *Sarah, Plain and Tall*
Shannon, George. *The Piney Woods Peddler*
Stevenson, James. *Wilfred the Rat*
Ward, Lynd. *The Biggest Bear*

CHALLENGING

Andersen, Hans Christian. *The Nightingale*
Anderson, Lonzo. *Arion and the Dolphins*

CHALLENGING (cont.) ════════════════════════

Hewitt, Kathryn. *The Three Sillies*
Steig, William. *Doctor De Soto*
Van Allsburg, Chris. *Jumanji*

ANDERSEN, Hans Christian. *The Nightingale.*   Illus. by Demi.
Harcourt, 1985. ISBN: 0-15-257427-1
The Chinese Emperor lived in a beautiful palace in a garden
filled with lovely colors and sounds. Beyond the garden is an
even larger forest. Visitors passing through the forest and garden
are awed by its beauty, and all believe that the most beautiful
sound is that of the nightingale that lives in the forest. Even the
Japanese Emperor is impressed by the bird's song. The Chinese
ruler must hear it and orders that the bird be brought to the palace. When the nightingale arrives and begins to sing, the music
is so lovely that the bird is asked to stay. Then a gift of a colorful
mechanical bird arrives from Japan. The new and the old birds
do not sing well together, so the real bird is exiled. Only when
the emperor is ill and the mechanical bird has broken do people
in the court realize the importance of the real nightingale.

Genre: Folklore
Subjects: Birds; folklore (Denmark); emperors; music
Award: *New York Times* Best Illustrated Children's Books
Award, 1987

ANDERSON, Lonzo. *Arion and the Dolphins.* Illus. by
Adrienne Adams. Scribner, 1978. ISBN: 0-684-15128-6 (o.s.i.)
Arion lived near the sea and would sit by the water and play
beautiful music. The dolphins came to love the music and the
music maker. When Arion wins a contest, he sails home with
gold; and others on board plot to rob and kill him. Only the dolphins can save Arion in this retelling of an ancient Greek leg-
end.

Genre: Folklore and fairy tales
Subject: Folklore (Greece)

COHEN, Barbara. *The Carp in the Bathtub.* Illus. by Joan
Halperin. Lothrop, 1972. ISBN: 0-688-51627-0
Leah comes home to find a giant fish in the bathtub. It is a carp
her mother has bought and is keeping for Passover, the Feast of
Seder. Leah and her brother, Harry, have other plans for the carp.

Having befriended the fish, they sneak it off to a neighbor for safekeeping. But grandmother knows, so the giant carp may still become fine gefilte fish to be eaten at the holiday dinner.

Genre: Realistic fiction
Subjects: Jewish Americans; carp

GOBLE, Paul. *The Girl Who Loved Wild Horses.* Illus. by the author. Bradbury, 1978. ISBN: 0-02-736570-0
An Indian girl watched the wild horses near her village every day until she fell in love with the beautiful animals. After they rescue her from a storm, she persuades her family that she must live among the horses, promising to return for a visit each year. Eventually, the maiden disappears and in her place there is the phantom of a new wild horse more beautiful than any of the others.

Genre: Adventure
Subjects: Native American Indians; horses
Award: Caldecott Medal Honor Books, 1979

GRAMATKY, Hardie. *Little Toot.* Illus. by the author. Putnam, 1939. ISBN: 0-399-60422-7
Little Toot is the smallest tugboat of them all. It has to work very hard to earn a place with the bigger boats; instead, the tugboat takes it easy. But then Little Toot is caught in a storm, and works in a way that wins it a high place among all the tugboats in the harbor. This is one in a series of books about Little Toot.

Genre: Fantasy
Subject: Tugboats

HEWITT, Kathryn. *The Three Sillies.* Illus. by the author. Harcourt, 1986. ISBN: 0-15-286855-0
A young man courting the farmer's daughter was surprised by her tearful behavior when she discovered an ax in the ceiling of the cellar. He was even more surprised when he found that the girl's parents acted in the same silly manner. The young man vowed to come back to marry the girl only when he had found three people sillier than they. During a long journey, the lad does find three people who do even sillier things than crying over an ax in the rafters.

Genre: Humor
Subject: Silliness

HOLABIRD, Katharine. *Angelina and the Princess.*   Illus. by Helen Craig. Clarkson Potter, 1984. ISBN: 0-517-55273-6
Just before the ballet tryouts, Angelina the mouse gets a cold. Her dancing is poor, and another dancer gets the lead part. The whole dance group works hard to perfect their performance for the princess. Angelina practices her own small part very diligently and even learns the lead part by herself. When the star is hurt just before the performance, only Angelina is prepared to take the role. She performs flawlessly, and the injured dancer is consoled by where she gets to sit. This is one in a series of books about Angelina the mouse ballerina.
Genre: Fantasy
Subjects: Mice; ballet; dancers

HOLABIRD, Katharine. *Angelina Ballerina.*   Illus. by Helen Craig. Clarkson Potter, 1983. ISBN: 0-517-55083-0
Angelina the mouse dreams about being a ballet dancer all the time. Unable to concentrate on the tasks at hand, she ruins some cheddar cheese pies with her gyrations and spills milk all over the kitchen. Finally, her father comes up with a solution — let Angelina take ballet lessons. His daughter is delighted and goes on to become a famous dancer. This is one in a series of books about Angelina the mouse.
Genre: Fantasy
Subjects: Mice; ballet

HURD, Edith Thacher. *I Dance in My Red Pajamas.*   Illus. by Emily Arnold McCully. Harper & Row, 1982. ISBN: 0-06-022699-4
Jenny's parents think she should quiet down when she visits her grandparents. But Grandpa is a little deaf and wants noise, not quiet. So Grandma plays the piano while Jenny dances in her red pajamas, stomping and clapping in her own loud way.
Genre: Realistic fiction
Subject: Grandparents

LASKER, Joe. *Nick Joins In.*   Illus. by the author. Whitman, 1980. ISBN: 0-8075-5612-2
Being in a wheelchair is awkward, but Nick decides that he won't let that stop him. He tries to do everything at school and is

discouraged because he can't play basketball. Nick watches the other boys play until one day there is a problem on the court that only Nick can solve.

Genre: Realistic fiction
Subjects: Physically handicapped; school stories; mainstreaming in education

MacLACHLAN, Patricia. *Sarah, Plain and Tall.* Illus. by the author. Harper & Row, 1985. ISBN: 0-06-024101-7
Calib and Anna live with their father in this story set in pioneer times. Their mother is gone and their father has ordered a new wife by mail order. Calib and Anna are worried about their new mother, who will arrive soon, and wonder what she will look like and how she will treat them. The new mother, Sarah, is plain and tall. She is also friendly, capable, and kind. Calib and Anna had wished she wasn't coming, but by the end of the story, they hope Sarah will stay forever.

Genre: Historical fiction
Subjects: Families; pioneer life; history

RASKIN, Ellen. *Spectacles.* Illus. by the author. Atheneum, 1968. ISBN: 0-689-20352-7
Iris Fogel did not want to wear glasses. But when she saw a fire-breathing dragon at the door, Iris's mother takes the girl to a "blue elephant," who prescribes glasses. Sharp pictures alternate with fuzzy ones to help establish Iris's need for glasses.

Genre: Realistic fiction
Subject: Eyeglasses
Award: *New York Times* Choice of Best Illustrated Children's Books of the Year, 1968

RYAN, Cheli Durán. *Hildilid's Night.* Illus. by Arnold Lobel. Macmillan, 1986. ISBN: 0-02-777260-8
Hildilid hates the night. She hates it so much she will try everything to get rid of it. All night long Hildilid chases the night, fans it away, carries bags of night away. Nothing works, and her efforts make her so weary that she is not at all ready for day when the night goes away. The detailed black-and-white sketches capture the silliness of Hildilid.

Genre: Humor
Subjects: Night; fear

SENDAK, Maurice. *Where the Wild Things Are.* Illus. by the author. Harper & Row, 1963. ISBN: 0-06-025520-X

When Max puts on his wolf suit, he begins to act like a wild animal. Soon his actions have gone too far and Max is sent to bed without supper. But his imagination is not dampened. His room soon becomes a forest near a large ocean that is complete with a ship. Max sails the ship to a strange land filled with unusual animals with yellow eyes. Fearlessly, Max tames the animals and becomes king of the forest. He treats his animal subjects just as he was treated at home, sending them to bed without supper. But finally, Max smells food and the fantasy comes to a comforting end.

Genre: Fantasy

Subjects: Boys; animals; imagination

SHANNON, George. *The Piney Woods Peddler.* Illus. by Nancy Tafuri. Greenwillow, 1981. ISBN: 0-688-80304-0

The peddler from Piney Woods works very hard but is a terrible businessman. He wants very much to give his daughter her wish for a present, a silver dollar. The trouble is that he has only his old horse to trade. Determined, the peddler sets out to sell or trade the horse and get the dollar. In the end he loses the horse and doesn't have the silver dollar. But the gift he does bring his daughter is something that she appreciates.

Genre: Realistic fiction

Subjects: Peddlers and peddling; families

STEIG, William. *Doctor De Soto.* Illus. by the author. Farrar, 1982. ISBN: 0-374-31803-4

Doctor De Soto is a mouse dentist, who doesn't usually take care of toothaches for big animals like the wolf. But this wolf is in great pain, so Dr. De Soto agrees to help. While he is working on the wolf, the wolf is planning to have the doctor for dinner. But Dr. De Soto and his nurse have a plan, too. With his new "painkiller," the doctor is able to close the wolf's mouth until everyone is safely out of reach.

Genre: Fantasy

Subjects: Dentists; mice

Award: Newbery Medal Honor Books, 1983

STEVENSON, James. *Wilfred the Rat.* Illus. by the author. Greenwillow, 1977. ISBN: 0-688-80103-1
Wilfred the rat was a lonely traveler until he fell asleep near the Ferris wheel in an amusement park. When he awoke, Wilfred found two great friends to have adventures with at the park. They tried everything together until Wilfred decided to show off his high-diving ability and performed a high dive that took him right into the popcorn.

Genre: Fantasy
Subjects: Animals; friendship

VAN ALLSBURG, Chris. *Jumanji.* Illus. by the author. Houghton Mifflin, 1981. ISBN: 0-395-30448-2
While walking in the park, Peter and Judy find a box with a game named Jumanji inside it. They decide to play Jumanji, which turns out to be an adventure game in which every choice becomes real. One problem leads to another until Peter and Judy are faced with a ferocious lion and have only one way to make it disappear. The almost photographic drawings add scary realism to the story.

Genre: Fantasy
Subject: Games
Awards: ALA Children's Notable Books, 1982; Caldecott Medal Honor Books, 1983

WARD, Lynd. *The Biggest Bear.* Illus. by the author. Houghton Mifflin, 1952. ISBN: 0-395-14806-5
Every barn in the valley has a bear skin hanging on it except Johnny Orchard's grandfather's place. Johnny decides he will have to do something about that and sets out to shoot the biggest bear of them all. However, Johnny's adventure takes a very different turn when he finds that the only bear on his trail is a baby cub.

Genre: Realistic fiction
Subject: Bears
Award: Caldecott Medal Honor Books, 1953

Appendix: Books in a Series

Many of the books chosen for this volume are parts of series. Because young people enjoy revisiting familiar characters, they may be challenged to read other books about them even though the readability level is more advanced. Listed here are books about those same characters. Those titles marked with an asterisk (*) appear in the body of this volume with full annotations. All the books listed here can easily be found in a public library.

Allard, Harry (Miss Nelson)
  Miss Nelson Has a Field Day
* Miss Nelson Is Back
* Miss Nelson Is Missing

Asch, Frank (Bear)
* Bear's Bargain
  Bear's Shadow
* Happy Birthday, Moon
* Just Like Daddy
* Moon Bear
* Mooncake
  Moongame
  Popcorn
* Sand Cake
  Skyfire

Bemelmans, Ludwig (Madeleine)
* Madeleine
  Madeleine and the Bad Hat
  Madeleine and the Gypsies
  Madeleine in London
* Madeleine's Rescue

Berenstain, Stan and Jan Berenstain (Berenstain Bears)
  (The Berenstains have written more than 20 other books about bears in the Berenstain Bears series.)
  The Bear Almanac
  The Bear Detectives
  Bears in the Night
* Bears on Wheels

Bond, Felicia (Poinsettia)
  Poinsettia and Her Family
* Poinsettia and the Firefighters

Brandenberg, Franz (Field mouse family)
* Everyone Ready?
* Nice New Neighbors
  Six New Students
  What Can You Make of It

Brandenberg, Franz (Leo and Emily)
* Leo and Emily

Brandenberg, Franz (cont.)
* Leo and Emily and the
  Dragon
* Leo and Emily's Big Ideas

Burningham, John (Mr.
  Gumpy)
* Mr. Gumpy's Motor Car
* Mr. Gumpy's Outing

Burningham, John (Shirley)
* Come Away from the Water,
  Shirley
  Time to Get Out of the Bath,
  Shirley

Calhoun, Mary (Henry the cat)
* Cross-Country Cat
* Hot Air Henry

Cohen, Miriam (Jim and his
  classmates)
  Bee My Valentine
  Best Friends
  First Grade Takes a Test
  Jim Meets the Thing
* Jim's Dog Muffins
  Liar, Liar Pants on Fire!
  Lost in the Museum
  The New Teacher
  No Good in Art
  Starring First Grade
* Tough Jim
  When Will I Read?

Delton, Judy (Duck, Bear, and
  their friends)
  Rabbit Finds a Way
  Three Friends Find Spring
* Two Good Friends
  Two Is Company

Dr. Seuss (The Cat in the Hat)
* The Cat in the Hat
* The Cat in the Hat Comes
  Back
* I Can Read with My Eyes
  Shut!

Duvoisin, Roger (Petunia)
* Petunia
  Petunia and the Song
  Petunia, Beware
* Petunia, I Love You
  Petunia Takes a Trip
  Petunia the Silly Goose Sto-
  ries
  Petunia's Christmas
  Petunia's Treasure

Goodall, John S. (Paddy Pork)
  Paddy Goes Traveling
* Paddy Pork—Odd Jobs
  Paddy Pork's Holiday
  Paddy to the Rescue
  Paddy under Water
  Paddy's Evening Out
  Paddy's New Hat

Gramatky, Hardie (Little Toot)
* Little Toot
  Little Toot on the Thames

Hoban, Lillian (Arthur)
* Arthur's Christmas Cookies
* Arthur's Funny Money
* Arthur's Halloween Costume
  Arthur's Honey Bear
  Arthur's Loose Tooth
  Arthur's New Power
  Arthur's Pen Pals
  Arthur's Prize Reader

Hoban, Russell (Frances)
  A Baby Sister for Frances
* A Bargain for Frances
* Bedtime for Frances
  Best Friends for Frances
  A Birthday for Frances
  Bread and Jam for Frances
  Egg Thoughts and Other
    Frances Soups

Hoff, Syd (Henrietta)
  Happy Birthday, Henrietta
  Henrietta Circus Star
* Henrietta Goes to the Fair
  Henrietta the Early Bird
* Henrietta's Fourth of July
  Henrietta's Halloween

Holabird, Katharine (Angelina)
  Angelina and Alice
* Angelina and the Princess
  Angelina at the Fair
* Angelina Ballerina
  Angelina on Stage
  Angelina's Christmas

Hughes, Shirley (Alfie)
* Alfie Gets in First
* Alfie Gives a Hand
* Alfie's Feet
* An Evening at Alfie's

Hutchins, Pat (Titch)
  Titch
* You'll Soon Grow into Them,
    Titch

Keats, Ezra Jack (Peter and his
    friends)
* Goggles
  Hi, Cat

* A Letter to Amy
  Pet Show
  Peter's Chair
* The Snowy Day
  Whistle for Willie

Kellogg, Steven (Pinkerton)
  Pinkerton, Behave
  Prehistoric Pinkerton
* A Rose for Pinkerton
  Tallyho, Pinkerton!

Lewis, Thomas P. (Mr. Sniff)
  Call for Mr. Sniff
* Mr. Sniff and the Motel Mys-
    tery

Lexau, Joan (Sam)
  I Should Have Stayed in Bed
* The Rooftop Mystery

Lobel, Arnold (Frog and Toad)
* Days with Frog and Toad
  Frog and Toad All Year
* Frog and Toad Are Friends
* Frog and Toad Together

Marshall, Edward (Fox)
  Fox All Week
* Fox and His Friends
  Fox at School
  Fox in Love
* Fox on Wheels

Marshall, James (George and
    Martha)
  George and Martha
* George and Martha, Back in
    Town
  George and Martha Encore

Marshall, James (cont.)
* George and Martha One Fine Day
* George and Martha, Rise and Shine
* George and Martha, Tons of Fun

Noble, Trinka Hakes (Jimmy's Boa)
* The Day Jimmy's Boa Ate the Wash
* Jimmy's Boa Bounces Back

Ormondroyd, Edward (Theodore)
* Theodore
  Theodore's Rival

Parish, Peggy (Amelia Bedelia)
  Amelia Bedelia
  Amelia Bedelia and the Baby
  Amelia Bedelia and the Surprise Shower
  Amelia Bedelia Goes Camping
* Amelia Bedelia Helps Out
  Come Back, Amelia Bedelia
  Good Work, Amelia Bedelia
  Merry Christmas, Amelia Bedelia
  Play Ball, Amelia Bedelia
  Teach Us, Amelia Bedelia
  Thank You, Amelia Bedelia

Platt, Kin (Big Max)
  Big Max
* Big Max in the Mystery of the Missing Moose

Quackenbush, Robert (Detective Mole)
  Detective Mole
* Detective Mole and the Circus Mystery
  Detective Mole and the Haunted Castle Mystery

Rey, H. A. (Curious George)
  (There are many books about Curious George; see also references under Rey, H. A. and Margaret Rey as well as Rey, Margaret and H. A. Rey.)
* Curious George
  Curious George Gets a Medal
  Curious George Learns the Alphabet
  Curious George Rides a Bike
  Curious George Takes a Job

Rey, H. A. and Margaret Rey (Curious George)
* Curious George Goes to the Hospital

Rey, Margaret and H. A. Rey (Curious George)
* Curious George Flies a Kite

Rylant, Cynthia (Henry and Mudge)
* Henry and Mudge: The First Book of Their Adventures
  Henry and Mudge in Puddle Trouble
  Henry and Mudge in the Green Time
  Henry and Mudge in the Sparkle Days

Henry and Mudge under a Yellow Moon

Schatell, Brian (Farmer Goff and Sam)
* Farmer Goff and His Turkey, Sam
* Sam's No Dummy, Farmer Goff

Sharmat, Marjorie Weinman (Nate the Great)
Nate the Great
Nate the Great and the Boring Beach Bag
Nate the Great and the Lost List
* Nate the Great and the Missing Key
Nate the Great and the Phony Clue
* Nate the Great and the Snowy Trail
* Nate the Great and the Sticky Case
Nate the Great Goes Undercover
Nate the Great Stalks Stupidweed

Stevenson, James (Grandpa and the grandchildren)
* Could Be Worse
Grandpa's Great City Tour: An Alphabet Book
The Great Big Especially Beautiful Easter Egg
No Friends
* That Dreadful Day

* That Terrible Halloween Night
There's Nothing to Do!
* We Can't Sleep
What's under My Bed?
Worse Than Willy!

Stevenson, James (Monty)
* Monty
No More Need for Monty

Turkle, Brinton (Obadiah)
* Obadiah the Bold
Rachel and Obadiah
Thy Friend Obadiah

Udry, Janice May (Mary Jo)
* What Mary Jo Shared
What Mary Jo Wanted

Van Leeuwen, Jean (Amanda Pig and Oliver Pig)
* Amanda Pig and Her Big Brother Oliver
More Tales of Amanda Pig
More Tales of Oliver Pig
Oliver, Amanda, and Grandmother Pig
Tales of Amanda Pig
Tales of Oliver Pig

Vincent, Gabrielle (Ernest and Celestine)
* Bravo, Ernest and Celestine!
Breakfast Time, Ernest and Celestine
* Ernest and Celestine
Ernest and Celestine's Patchwork Quilt
Ernest and Celestine's Picnic

Vincent, Gabrielle (cont.)
* Merry Christmas, Ernest and Celestine
* Smile, Ernest and Celestine
  Where Are You, Ernest and Celestine?

Waber, Bernard (Lyle)
* The House on East 88th Street
  Lovable Lyle
  Lyle and the Birthday Party
  Lyle Finds His Mother
* Lyle, Lyle, Crocodile

Watanabe, Shigeo (young bear)
  Daddy Play with Me
* How Do I Put It On?
* I Can Build a House!
* I Can Ride It!
  I Can Take a Bath!
  I Can Take a Walk!
  I'm the King of the Castle!
  What a Good Lunch!
  Where's My Daddy?

Wells, Rosemary (Max)
  Max's Bath
  Max's Bedtime
  Max's Birthday
  Max's Breakfast
  Max's Christmas
* Max's First Word
* Max's New Suit
  Max's Ride
  Max's Toys: A Counting Book

Wheeler, Cindy (Marmalade)
  Marmalade's Christmas Present
* Marmalade's Nap
* Marmalade's Picnic
  Marmalade's Snowy Day
* Marmalade's Yellow Leaf

Williams, Vera B. (Rosa and her family)
* A Chair for My Mother
* Music, Music for Everyone
* Something Special for Me

Wiseman, Bernard (Morris and Boris)
  Christmas with Morris and Boris
  Halloween with Morris and Boris
* Morris and Boris
* Morris Goes to School
  Morris Has a Birthday Party!
* Morris Has a Cold
* Morris Tells Boris Mother Moose Stories and Rhymes

Zion, Gene (Harry the dog)
  Harry and the Lady Next Door
  Harry by the Sea
* Harry the Dirty Dog
  No Roses for Harry

Subject Index

Two guides have been used in the selection of the topic headings: the Library of Congress Subject Headings and the children in our group. An asterisk (*) precedes those subjects that the children in our group most often selected. We feel that these subjects hold the most interest to children.

Readability Index

Author Index

Title Index